Bill,
   This book highlights
the Christian mission
in many Y's.
   Great seeing you
at the US mission
Network conference.

          Bruce Bryn

TOUCHPOINTS OF FAITH
GOD'S WORD IN DAILY LIFE

TOUCHPOINTS OF FAITH
GOD'S WORD IN DAILY LIFE

BRUCE BOYER

Published by
Alabaster Book Publishing
North Carolina

Published by Alabaster Book Publishing
P.O. Box 401
Kernersville, North Carolina 27285
www.PublisherAlabaster.biz

Book design by
D.L.Shaffer

Cover photo by
Bruce Boyer and Gene Stafford

First Edition

ISBN: 978-0-9861790-9-9

Library of Congress Control Number
2016914013

Acknowledgements

All my life I have been surrounded by people of faith who inspired me to strengthen my own faith. Most of my career I have worked for the Christian-based YMCA. The acronym YMCA stands for Young Men's Christian Association. The combination of being surrounded by people of faith and the opportunity to share my faith daily through the YMCA increased my desire to serve the Lord.

During my youth at YMCA resident camp The Old Gray Goose was the biggest influence on my career choice to be a YMCA director. My first devotional book, 24/7: Stories of Faith from Everyday Life, was dedicated to Goose. One of his legendary stories is included in this book.

For the past 37 years I have had the good fortune to play a role in the broader YMCA mission movement. God orchestrated each step of the way. I just said, *"Here am I, send me" (Isaiah 6:8)* and He provided the opportunities. In 1979 I received a mailing about a Christian training event at the Long Beach (CA) YMCA camp, Camp Oakes. My Ohio camp couldn't afford to send me to a conference in California, but somehow I mustered up the courage to ask for financial assistance to attend. Undoubtedly it was the Holy Spirit at work, urging me to take the first step. The CJ, Carrie D. and R. Howard Walker Foundation, which was unknown to me at the time, paid my entire way: travel expenses and conference fees. The Walker foundation sponsors this conference each year as a memorial to Howard Walker, a family member who lost his life in a farming accident. The purpose of the Christian Leadership Conference is to train the camp's summer staff in how to put Christian values in their program. At that 1979 conference the Holy Spirit spoke to me again, this time giving me the courage to ask Ken Walker, Howard's father, to fund a similar conference at my YMCA camp in Columbus, Ohio. He did. The Ohio CLC started a domino effect with the Walker Foundation funding conferences at YMCA's all across the country. Ken Walker's generosity sparked a passion in me to host Christian Leadership conferences at every YMCA I worked at for the remainder of my career. Now retired, I have represented the Walker Foundation at CLCs nationally. Many of the guest authors in this book are volunteers for the foundation and National CLC Director Terra Lynn Dearth is also a guest author. She tells the story of the Walker family, why they created Christian Leadership conferences, and how they have been instrumental in keeping the YMCA grounded in the faith.

I am grateful for YMCA directors Rosemary Suess and Derek Edwards (YMCA of Northwest North Carolina), who dedicated countless hours evaluating and helping select the stories for this book. They served as advisors for the content of this book. Rosemary Suess directs the most mission-driven YMCA I have ever experienced. She, the Walker Foundation and the eleven guest authors were the inspiration to dedicate this book to the Christian mission of the YMCA. God is truly at work through their efforts at the YMCA.

Each of the guest authors provided a story for this book. Prior to each story there is a brief introduction of their role in keeping "the C" strong in the YMCA. Guest authors are **Cliff Christian** (YMCA Blue Ridge Assembly), **Terra Lynn Dearth** (National Director for Christian Leadership Conferences and the Rags & Leathers Program), **Dan Doctor** (school administrator and Walker Foundation volunteer), **Eric Ellsworth** (YMCA of Greater Indianapolis CEO), **The Old Gray Goose** (legendary YMCA storyteller), **Bruce Ham** (YMCA of the Triangle), **Bob Kahle** (YMCA camp director), **Gray Stallworth** (recently retired YMCA Executive Director from Greenwood, SC), **Rosemary Suess** (Executive Director, YMCA of Northwest North Carolina), **Bob Warnock** (retired YMCA camp executive), and **Larry Whittlesey** (National Director for the US Mission Network). I am humbled these friends were willing to be part of my devotional book.

Family friends Jeff Shu and Lisa Shu helped proofread this book. Chris van der Horst, another family friend, reviews my weekly devotions I email out each week. I am also grateful to website developer Rich Blakemore for helping me put together an internet site, www.ChristianFaithStories.com, to post new stories each week as a continuation of my ministry. The general public can download these weekly devotional stories.

The real source of story ideas is the Holy Spirit. I am convinced that God continually places in my path events and interactions where I can see Him at work. They have become the basis for my story ministry. As I live my life, the Holy Spirit keeps me tuned into how faith is part of my daily life. God is the center of my life. I do my best to listen for his direction every day and then to utilize publications and electronic communication to share the Gospel through easy-to-understand stories.

Dedication

Outdoor Chapel at the Kernersville
Family YMCA

I dedicate this devotional book to the Christian mission of the YMCA. In keeping with The Great Commission, the YMCA is uniquely positioned to share the Gospel of Jesus Christ in the community.

Therefore go and make disciples of all nations, baptizing them in the name of the Father and of the Son and of the Holy Spirit, and teaching them to obey everything I have commanded you. And surely I am with you always, to the very end of the age (Matthew 28:19-20).

The Why Behind the Y Mission

Being a YMCA professional director for 34 years, I chose a Y career because of its Christian mission. This devotional book contains stories from 11 guest authors who also embrace the YMCA as their ministry.

The nation's largest non-profit organization is very familiar as most communities are blessed to have a YMCA. The Young Men's Christian Association came to the United States in 1851 after originating in London, England. Today's YMCA has three key focus areas:

- Youth Development

- Healthy Living

- Social Responsibility

These focus areas underscore the priority of investing in our kids, our health, and our communities. I view these focus areas as "walking the talk" of the Y's Christian mission. It is not enough to merely be of faith, but to do something about it. We serve God by serving others and we hope our actions encourage others in the faith. *In the same way, let your light shine before others, that they may see your good deeds and glorify your Father in heaven (Matthew 5:16).*

Youth Development spotlights nurturing the potential of every child and teen; Healthy Living aims to improve the nation's health and well-being; Social Responsibility urges us to give back and provide support to our neighbors. As we all know, doing good deeds is not enough. At the center of our good works is the faith that motivates us to show our love for others.

The Y's national mission statement states, "To put Christian principles into practice through programs that build healthy spirit, mind and body for all." The Y inspires us to base our lives on Christian principles. A key part of the mission statement is depicted in the equilateral triangle in the Y's logo. The Y believes in the equal development of a person spiritually, mentally, and physically. Because of Christian values people learn to make good decisions and to develop their minds to help maximize their potential. Everyone recognizes the Y's role in the community aims also to develop good health habits through exercise and proper nutrition.

God created man in His own image. Just as there are three persons of God – Father, Son, and Holy Spirit – mankind has 3 parts as well – spirit, mind, and body. *May God himself, the God of peace, sanctify you through and through. May your whole spirit, soul and body be kept blameless at the coming of our Lord Jesus Christ (1 Thessalonians 5:23).*

The YMCA is ideally positioned as a community service organization. It is where the community comes together for a common purpose. YMCAs serve the entire population, including all ages, nationalities, faiths, and economic levels. It grants full participation to the disadvantaged by giving the more fortunate a means to invest in their community by helping the needy. *The King will reply, 'Truly I tell you, whatever you did for one of the least of these brothers and sisters of mine, you did for me' (Matthew 25:40).* As an organization the Y is often the most benevolent investor in serving the needy. My own home YMCA matches the contributions of others with its own resources to help twice as many needy people.

The Y originated as a Bible study organization in 1844. Twenty-two year old English businessman Sir George Williams was concerned that young men moving to the city needed guidance. The Industrial Revolution attracted people to the city in search of employment, taking them away from their families. The program of the first YMCA was Bible study, conducted in an upper room above a London, England department store. This effort provided God's Word and a positive role model so that young men would avoid the temptations of the city.

Over the years the Y has been at the forefront of new ideas based on needs of each generation. The Y very quickly became a global organization with a significant impact on its communities. The Y continued to be responsive to changing needs as our country experienced change. Let me give a few examples.

In the early 1900s the YMCA highlighted the culture of the American Indian adult male's significant involvement in raising of young boys in their families. This is contrasted with the American culture where the father went to work and left the mother to raise the children. This program was at the root of 20th century family program initiatives. Developing a program where the father spent quality time with his children became the model for one of the largest programs in YMCA history: Y-Indian Guides and Y-Indian Princesses. I remember my own daughter, riding in the car with me on a family errand, saying "Dad, this is like Indian Princesses. It's just you and me." The one-on-one time together through the YMCA was priceless.

- During the Civil War the YMCA focused efforts on assisting troops and prisoners of war, providing over 1 million Bibles to both sides of the conflict.

- Y staff and volunteers went to Europe to help care for prisoners of war in both world wars. The YMCA helped establish USO services for those in the military.

- The Atlanta Y was a meeting place for Dr. Martin Luther King as he successfully sought to bring dignity to African Americans.

- Sports such as basketball, volleyball, and racquetball were YMCA inventions, and the YMCA was the pioneer of indoor swimming pools.

- As far back as 1914 YMCA overnight camps began programs to encourage campers and staff to accept challenges for self-improvement. The faith-based Rags & Leathers program has a 100-year history of encouraging people in the faith. A second initiative involved staff training events that focus on Christian values in all aspects of the YMCA. Christian Leadership Conferences have been held nationwide since 1974, primarily funded by the C.J., Carrie D. & R. Howard Walker Foundation (Long Beach, California), a family foundation dedicated to the YMCA mission movement.

- Perhaps the most famous YMCA director was John R. Mott, who was awarded the Nobel Peace Prize in 1946 for his work in lay ministry. Through the YMCA Mott helped establish the World Council of Churches, the World Student Christian Federation and the Student Volunteer Movement for Foreign Missions.

- Lately, the YMCA has initiated the US Mission Network, an effort to equip top level YMCA leadership through spiritual development. Christian emphasis doesn't happen without intentional efforts to inspire and train Y leadership.

The list goes on and on, but the bottom line is the Y has been innovative and responsive to community needs throughout its history, driven by the foundation of its Christian purpose.

The core of the Y's historic logo shows an open Bible highlighting the verse *John 17:21*. The verse encourages all people to be one with the Father. *That all of them may be one, Father, just as you are in me and I am in you. May they also be in us so that the world may believe that you have sent me (John 17:21).*

Although many Y's are abundant in wellness and athletic facilities, you can also see Y's to be intentional in sharing the Gospel. Prayer breakfasts, scripture verses posted on fitness equipment and in gymnasiums, and indoor and outdoor chapels at the Y are consistent with the modern focus areas of Youth Development, Healthy Living, and Social Responsibility. Spiritual development is at the core of all three focus areas. God has blessed this organization because it is doing great things in His name.

As you can see from this brief overview, God has enabled the YMCA to share the Gospel in the community. Today's modern focus areas are ways the Y puts faith into action by serving our communities and improving God's temple, our bodies. No organization does it better.

Table of Contents

Faith Lessons with a Seasonal Topic

Introduction

Living Faith: It is critically important we learn to apply our faith to our everyday lives. Being a Christian is not just attending church on Sunday morning. Being a person of faith is more than believing there is a God, but understanding how He works in our daily lives. Being a Christian means establishing a personal relationship to Jesus Christ so that He is part of our everyday lives. Most of the stories in this book were written over a two-year period, giving a real-time accounting of the ups and downs of my life. During the past two years my family experienced the blessed birth of three grandchildren and our daughter's wedding. I have enjoyed new meaningful friendships and rewarding volunteer roles in the community. God has been very good to me. I also experienced the passing of my father and father-in-law, both well into their 90's. All of these events, good and bad, are depicted in some way in this book.

Format of Stories: The approach of my devotional books is to share the Good News in a way that makes sense to people. I present stories with which people can identify, and then relate a faith lesson to each story. Once someone understands the context of a story, they can see God at work in their life. Concluding each story with a question brings you into the story. Each story also includes at least one scriptural reference to show the lesson is not just good moral behavior, but God's answer.

Similar to Parables of the Bible: Many lessons of the Bible are taught through parables, providing common ground and a familiar starting point to His teachings. Parables have been called "earthly stories with a heavenly meaning." Through the use of parables, people can better understand the character of God and His expectations for us. Jesus' parables allow people to see the storyline from a third-party perspective. Only after a person decides what the right answer is, Jesus turns the tables and places the listener into the story. At that point Jesus tells people the story is really about them. It is easy making decisions on how other people should act when it doesn't affect you; but once you can see yourself in the story, you more deeply feel its impact.

Memorable Stories: A major goal for teaching through stories is to create a memorable lesson. Let me give you an example. This book contains the story "Never Mind, Lord." I heard that story at Hope Congregational Church in Springfield, Massachusetts, when I was a college student in the late 1960s. Pastor (Dr.) Charles Warren Barnes told a story about a little boy on the roof of his house, as part of a sermon. The boy started to slide down the roof and asked God for help. Just before tumbling to the ground below his pants caught on a nail, and he was safe. The boy said, "Never mind Lord. I am OK now." I still remember the story and lesson today, nearly 50 years later. If Dr. Barnes had merely preached a sermon that God answers our prayers I probably would have forgotten the point of his sermon by lunch time that day. But I remember it because of the context of a story. The lesson stuck with me for half century. People remember stories better than just a one-line directive. It is my hope and prayer that the faith lessons of this book will stick with you because they are integrated into real-life stories.

Desired End Result: The Apostle Paul's approach was that whatever we teach should be simply stated and understandable by those who don't yet know Christ. For that reason I have avoided using phrases only familiar to people who attend church regularly. By keeping it simple it is my hope that more people may come to faith as a result. *And the Lord added to their number daily those who were being saved (Acts 2:47).*

Feature Story:

Turning It Over To God

The feature story of this devotional book talks about a key turning point in my YMCA career. I was facing a year with several make-or-break variables, all at the same time. I was scared. My career depended on being successful with opening a major facility expansion to an older building. The key part of the challenge was the membership rate was going up significantly, overnight. Would the community abandon the YMCA for less expensive facilities in the area? My YMCA was always a Christian mission-oriented YMCA, but somewhat on my terms. My solution was I turned over my YMCA over to God. The story, "Turning It Over to God", shows how God responded. God has been #1 at my YMCA ever since.

Bruce Boyer

Topic: My Personal Story

Turning It Over to God?

My YMCA had just completed a major addition to the facility, significantly enhancing the quality of equipment and square footage. The facility had been transformed from an aging building with antiquated equipment to something our members could be really proud of. The transformation also meant membership rates would need to reflect the enhanced value of the facility, and would be needed to pay off some of the remaining construction costs. In addition, we were consolidating membership categories, so a larger than usual membership rate increase was warranted. The new facilities would open the first of the year. As I completed the budget I had knots in my stomach. What if the membership rebelled against the new rates? What if they quit and went to other facilities? Would I still have a job if we were not successful in maintaining our members in spite of the large rate increase?

To protect myself I built a very conservative budget very tight on the expenses, and actually projecting a decrease in membership. I got approval for the budget but had reservations on how the community would react. My community had a reputation for being very cost sensitive. I had reason to worry.

As year-end approached I tried to focus my attention on the celebration of the Christmas season. Christmas that year was with my family, some 16 hours' drive away. We packed up the car for the all-night drive. During the long drive my mind drifted back and forth between the upcoming celebration of the birth of the Christ child and my concern for fiscal responsibility in the coming year.

I had the early morning shift behind the wheel while my family slept in route to our Christmas celebration. It was during that 2 AM uninterrupted quiet time with God that I turned the corner – not onto any highway, but into a mindset of peace. What gave me the sense of peace? I ended my mental torture by turning my YMCA over to God. It was a very intentional prayer. The Kernersville Family YMCA was now His YMCA. I was just the hands that did the daily work, and I did it for Him. From that moment on God took on my burdens and worries. I made a promise to God. I pledged I would do everything I could to make my YMCA a Godly YMCA. I would listen to Him to understand what He wanted me to do. By the time my shift at the wheel ended I was at peace. It was God's YMCA now. For the first time in weeks I could sleep in peace, not worrying about the financial success of my YMCA come January 1.

How did things turn out? The line to sign up for memberships at the New Year's open house was out the door. The public embraced the better facilities and were willing to pay the larger membership fee. Instead of a 40% loss in number of members that year, we gained 40%. We exceeded budget every month, which meant we could pay off the construction costs at a faster pace, and restore the budget cuts I had made. We offered the community a better YMCA – not only in quality of facilities but in its Christian mission.

As a result of this transformation my YMCA developed the reputation of being a Christian YMCA, a reputation that continues to this day. We coordinated area churches for the community prayer breakfast, stepped up Christian signage throughout the building, opened a Christian library in our lobby area and increased Christian emphasis into every program we offered. Both God and staff each kept up their part of the pledge for the Kernersville Family YMCA to be a place where God is the head of our organization.

I have sought for every YMCA where I am affiliated to be a Christian YMCA, but I had never before pledged to God I would do everything He asked me to do. Previously, it was my best guess of what I *thought* God wanted from me. This time I asked. This took us to a much higher level of Christian service.

The Kernersville YMCA is living proof that God blesses us bountifully if we ask. He certainly blessed my YMCA and me, personally, as I sought to do His Will.

Let God be the master of your life and work. Pledge to God that you will make wherever you work a place for Christian fellowship, love, learning, and achievement.

Scripture: *The Lord bless you and keep you; the Lord make his face shine on you and be gracious to you; the Lord turn his face toward you and give you peace (Numbers 6:24-26).*

Commit to the Lord whatever you do, and he will establish your plans (Proverbs 16:3).

Question: Are you willing to turn your success over to God?

Prayer: Dear Lord, we know You will bless our efforts when we seek to serve You. Amen.

Bruce Boyer

Faith Stories from Everyday Life

Stories for personal reading or as a group
devotional at the beginning of a meeting or event.

Topic: Afterlife

Loss or Lost?

I have a habit of getting lost when driving on unfamiliar roads. I know where I want to go, but often turn the wrong way if I don't have directions. The term "lost" is not much of a stretch when I am traveling.

My father passed away at the age of 99. At the funeral home visitation many people said they were "sorry for your loss." It was a very appropriate statement to make, knowing we would miss Dad very much. We are a close-knit family. But if people had said Dad was "lost," the statement would be completely false. We know exactly where Dad is, both physically and spiritually. Dad's body is resting at White Haven Memorial Park next to Mom. His soul, however, is in Heaven with Jesus. He certainly is not lost. Scripture tells us, Dad is in the presence of Jesus Christ and will be reunited with loved ones of the faith. He already has been reunited with Mom.

People without a relationship to Jesus Christ have a totally different story. They *are* lost. They need direction to find their way.

As Christians we have the opportunity to help other people avoid being lost. We can encourage people to welcome Jesus into their lives so they will experience God's Grace and Mercy. We do this in a gentle, loving way, just as Jesus did. If someone is not ready, be patient and hopeful they will eventually accept God into their life. Ask God to give you guidance on how to reach someone. Our role is to soften hearts by being an example of how God's love has changed us. We plant seeds, and when people are ready, the Holy Spirit then works its magic.

Scripture: *Therefore, since we have been made right in God's sight by faith, we have peace with God because of what Jesus Christ our Lord has done for us (Romans 5:1).*

Question: How do you encourage others to accept Jesus Christ into their lives?

Prayer: Dear Lord, we know You offer eternal life to all believers who ask forgiveness for their sins. Help us to influence others to accept You into their lives. Amen.

Additional Verses about God's Grace and Mercy

Mercy:
- *For the wages of sin is death, but the gift of God is eternal life in Christ Jesus our Lord (Romans 6:23).*
- *And I saw the dead, great and small, standing before the throne, and books were opened. Another book was opened, which is the book of life. The dead were judged according to what they had done as recorded in the books. The sea gave up the dead that were in it, and death and Hades gave up the dead that were in them, and each person was judged according to what they had done. Then death and Hades were thrown into the lake of fire. The lake of fire is the second death. Anyone whose name was not found written in the book of life was*

thrown into the lake of fire (Rev. 20:12-15).
- *Have mercy on me, O God, according to your unfailing love; according to your great compassion blot out my transgressions. Wash away all my iniquity and cleanse me from my sin (Psalms 51:1-2).*

Grace:
- *But because of his great love for us, God, who is rich in mercy, made us alive with Christ even when we were dead in transgressions—it is by grace you have been saved (Ephesians 2:4-5).*
- *For all have sinned and fall short of the glory of God, and all are justified freely by his grace through the redemption that came by Christ Jesus (Romans 3:23-24).*

Our Response:
- *Let us then approach God's throne of grace with confidence, so that we may receive mercy and find grace to help us in our time of need (Hebrews 4:16).*

Topic: Assurance

Investment Report

Like many adults, I receive a monthly statement of my investments, allowing me to track financial goals. Sometimes the statements are encouraging while other times just the opposite. Either way the results largely are beyond my control.

During times of declining stock values there are usually unsettling world or national events that affect consumer confidence in the market. Sometimes simple fear of an upcoming event causes stock prices to tumble. Other times we are told it is just a market adjustment. Yet, investment advisors usually tell us not to panic. History clearly shows the market generally improves over time, yielding a long-term positive gain.

How are you doing with the investment in your faith? God doesn't send you a written report but if you reflected for a quiet moment you could assess whether or not you are in a positive relationship with your Heavenly Father, today. Just like the stock market, confidence in your own faith can wobble based on what is happening in your life. Situations beyond your control often affect the strength of your faith at any given moment. When the uncertainty of employment or relationships affects us personally, we sometimes pull back from our faith, the one thing that could help us most in difficult times. We often let the enormity of our despair overcome us, letting outside influences control our personal relationship with our Heavenly Father.

During difficult times we should take the investment advisor's advice to stay the course. Have confidence that God will see you through the difficult times and bring you out on the other side in a stronger position. Make a conscious effort to strengthen your faith, especially during the difficult times. Your friends, your church, and your family are all positioned to support you as you deal with disappointment, but the most important spiritual advisor is God.

Investment counselors tell us to maintain our investments in the market even when it is down. In fact, when the market is down, the time is right for a greater investment. We should do the same with our faith. There is no better time to tap into God's strength than when we need it the most.

It takes commitment to stay the course with our faith when times are tough. Just like looking at one investment report, we put too much stock in a snapshot of a single moment in time. History tells us there is a positive gain ahead. God has assured us: *Surely, I am with you always, to the very end of the age (Matthew 28:20)*. Stay strong in the faith throughout the good times and the bad, and God will reward you. God is with you every day, assuring you of success for the long haul.

Someday you will be able to retire in heaven.

Scripture: *"Though the mountains be shaken and the hills be removed,* *yet my unfailing love for you will not be shaken, nor my covenant of peace be removed," says the Lord, who has compassion on you (Isaiah 54:10).*

Question: When times get tough, do you stay true to your faith?

Prayer: Dear Lord, every day presents new challenges, with victories and disappointments. We know we can rely on You to carry us through the disappointments. We will stay the course of our faith. Amen.

Topic: Blessings

Clear and Sunny
Means Trouble is Ahead

 The airplane touched down in Rochester, New York, delivering me for a late October weekend visit with family. Typical Rochester temperatures at that time of year hover around 60 degrees, but that particular Friday afternoon the weather was 75 degrees and sunny. It was a beautiful day. Things couldn't be better. At least, so it seemed.

Two days later it was time for the return trip home. The unseasonably warm Friday weather was a fluke. Hurricane Sandy had pushed the better than usual weather ahead of the turbulent front that was to follow. The entire East Coast was in the line of fire for hurricane winds, flooding, and even heavy snow. By Sunday afternoon most of the Eastern Seaboard airports had closed and planes were being sent elsewhere. Some 12,500 flights were cancelled from Sunday afternoon to Monday. New York City shut down its subway system. Eventually, most of the tunnels leading into the city were flooded, as were the closed subway tunnels, some of the worst devastation New York City had experienced. Whatever happened to the perfect weather we enjoyed on Friday?

It reality, it was a "perfect storm" of atmospheric conditions. The hurricane born in the South Atlantic collided with two other weather systems to create unbelievable havoc. On top of that, the full moon meant that the tides were at their peak power. As a result, rivers and the Atlantic coastline reached higher water levels than have been seen before. A state of emergency was declared in most of the Eastern part of the U.S.

Life has a way of laying some of our biggest problems in the wake of euphoric times. When things are going well we tend to enjoy the moment, and forget to include God in our lives. We're doing just fine on our own, we think. Then disaster strikes, creating our own state of emergency.

How do we handle the good times?

During those euphoric times, thank God for the blessings that made things so good for you. Appreciate what God has done for you. When times are good, it is God blessing you. Don't forget him at times of euphoric joy, as the good in your life is a gift from God. Stay close to God, knowing that storms may be just over the horizon, waiting to strike when you least expect it.

During those good times Satan is trying to make you feel like it was your accomplishment that brought on the good times, and you really don't need God. Who needs God when things are going well? You do! If you keep close to God at all times you will be ready for even the Perfect Storm of life.

We all know that life can't always be sunny skies and 75 degrees.

We're not in heaven yet.   But remaining in the faith, we can trust that our God will raise us up above the disasters that we will face during those difficult times.

Scripture: *Give thanks in all circumstances, for this is God's will for you in Christ Jesus (1 Thessalonians 5:18).*

Question: When things are going well, how do you resist the temptation to take credit for God's blessings?

Prayer: We pray, Lord, that we never take Your many blessings for granted. When times are good, we know You are at the controls, providing for our needs. These are the times when we want to build a relationship so that we can work together to handle the tough times.

Topic: Choices

Final Answer?

One of the more popular daytime television game shows is called, Who Wants to Be a Millionaire? Contestants who answer all the questions can win $1 million. To make it easier, four possible answers are provided. Just pick the right one every time and you win the $1 million prize. The show even provides lifelines – the opportunity to phone a friend, ask the audience or eliminate half the choices. Sounds easy.

On closer examination, typically two of the answers on the board are very similar, and designed to make the contestant second guess themselves. One is the right answer and the other a deceptive suggestion designed to trip up the contestant.

Unlike many other game shows, the contestants are given ample time to select their answers. Contestants start to rationalize their choice as they narrow down their options. After much deliberation, the contestants give their answers. To be sure everyone is clear on the chosen answer, the contestant is asked if that is their "final answer." Once the contestant says "final answer," there is no going back. Then, the host makes the contestant squirm a little before revealing if the final answer is right.

Thankfully, we don't have to answer important questions of life under the bright lights of the television camera, watched by a nationwide viewing audience, second guessing our choices. Not only are the lights intended to illuminate the set, but also to intimidate the contestant.

When facing difficult issues in our lives, we also have lifelines. We live in an environment where we constantly evaluate our choices compared to worldly norms, which is like asking the audience. With a sizeable part of the population unchurched, that could be a recipe for disaster. We have friends we can consult, but if they are not of faith, their answers will be their own worldly opinions rather than God's answers. Taking away half of the wrong answers still leave us with a choice to make, and only one right answer. You could exhaust all your lifelines and still get the wrong answer. In the end, it depends on who is guiding you and how much you trust

their answers. Worldly questions may win you $1 million. Answering God's questions correctly means winning much more.

When the Romans nailed Jesus to the cross, they were seeking an end to His ministry. They wanted to silence him who was causing people to look to God for answers instead of the Roman rulers. The Romans were afraid the King of the Jews would lessen their power over their subjects. They didn't understand the concept of God's kingdom.

While the Roman rulers thought the crucifixion was the final answer, it wasn't. God's final answer was the Resurrection – Jesus rising from the dead in victory over evil. God's kingdom cannot be won or bought at any human price. Jesus paid the price for us. To reach the final question we have a number of questions to answer. How are we going to show our love for Jesus Christ? Do we believe Jesus is our Lord and Savior? Do we believe He died for our sins? Are we sorry (repent) for our sins? We have to get all of the earlier questions right to reach the final question: what happens to me when I pass from this earth. God will provide the final answer. And it is priceless.

Questions: How do we show our love for Jesus Christ? Do we believe Jesus is our Lord and Savior? Do we believe He died for our sins? Are we sorry and repentant for our sins?

Scripture: *If you confess with your mouth, "Jesus is Lord," and believe in your heart that God raised Him from the dead, you will be saved (Romans 10:9).*

Prayer: Lord, there are many people who want to convince us to follow earthly ways. But You provide the truth that salvation comes to those who believe. We pray we will turn to You for the final answer. Amen.

Topic: Christian Community

A Village Plays Salvation – A Commitment Fulfilled

 Every 10 years the village of Oberammergau, Germany, puts on a summer season of the Passion Play. The production is a fulfillment of a pledge made by this community in 1633, nearly 380 years ago. At the time of the pledge, the plague that had been killing millions in Europe was threatening the village of Oberammergau. In Medieval times there was no cure for this highly contagious disease: contracting it was a death sentence. The community promised God that if He would spare their village they would portray the "Passion, Death and Resurrection of our Lord, Jesus Christ" to the world. The first production was held in 1634, and is currently offered to a world-wide audience every 10 years.

The show is a live re-enactment of the events of Holy Week, starting with Jesus' triumphal entry into Jerusalem on Palm Sunday and concluding with the resurrection.

So how did the pledge work out? God has protected the village. No one from the community has succumbed to the Black Death. During the two world wars, the community was never hit by bombing raids that destroyed much of Germany.

What is remarkable is the commitment of the *entire community* to uphold a pledge made by their village centuries ago. Of the 5,000 current town residents, half are involved in the show, with 2,000 performing as actors, singers and musicians in the orchestra. Other townspeople work behind the scenes. No one is brought in from the outside to assist this production. Even the woodcarver from whom we purchased souvenirs was due at the theatre 30 minutes after we visited his shop, and we saw him on stage. It was an unbelievably high quality production.

In Oberammergau, *everyday people* were upholding a promise to God. We know God upholds His promise to us. God saw a community come together in faith and commit themselves to share the Good News with others. As a result, the village remains healthy and is thriving today.

Now look at your community and your role in keeping it healthy and thriving. Is there a unity of purpose in your community – perhaps a goal of being a wholesome, family community? We don't need to be threatened by a devastating health crisis to pledge to God that we will share his message with others. We can do that because Jesus wanted us to spread the Good News to people of all nations. Make a commitment to God that you will do your part to strengthen your community as a community of faith. Ask someone to go to church and encourage others to grow in their faith. Just as the village of Oberammergau found, there are roles everyone in the community can play. And God will reward the effort.

Scripture: *He always stands by his covenant—the commitment he made to a thousand generations (Psalm 105:8).*

Question: How can you play a role in your community so that it will be known as a wholesome, family community that reflects Christian values?

Prayer: Dear Lord, we commit ourselves to do our part to make our community a wholesome community, sharing God's Word with others. Amen.

Bruce Boyer

Extraordinary Christian Leadership

Think back to a supervisor who exhibited extraordinary Christian leadership. It probably was a time when you felt strong, caring support and grew the most as a person. You felt appreciated and valued, and that your supervisor really cared about you as a person. The well-being of your family was important to the supervisor. Coming to work as an employee or volunteer was fun because of the family atmosphere of the workplace.

This is the leadership style Jesus utilized in training His disciples for the ministry. Jesus knew his time on earth was limited. He needed to give significant attention to His disciples so they would be ready to carry out the ministry after He was gone. The future success of the ministry depended on the preparation and development of His team.

An excellent book entitled <u>The Master Plan of Evangelism</u> outlines Jesus' leadership style. The book is intended to lay out a plan for training leaders to do evangelical work for their church, but its principles are valid to prepare leaders in other fields as well. It provides a wonderful plan for Christian leadership much needed in today's pressure-packed world.

A Christian leader demonstrates their faith through their actions. You can trust their decisions because their strength and direction comes from God. Their guidebook is the scriptures. Christian leaders are willing to roll up their sleeves and do any task they ask others to do. They are sacrificial with their own time so that their employees and volunteers can have relief when it is needed. Noted Christian author A.W. Tozer wrote, "No man gives anything acceptable to God until he has first given himself in love and sacrifice." Everything the Christian leader does is because God loved us first.

The Christian leader doesn't need the biggest office or best seat at the table, just the biggest heart. *I am the good shepherd. The good shepherd lays down his life for the sheep (John 10:11).* Their entire life is a living witness of putting others before self.

They develop others by giving clear direction and check in often to review progress and offer guidance. They don't micro-manage but they are there to support when needed. They expect their employee's best efforts, but because they know their employees well, they know their current and future capabilities. Christian leaders genuinely care more about the individual than the task at hand. The old adage, "People don't care what you know until they know you care," is absolutely true. The result of following this principle wins the loyalty of employees and volunteers.

The Christian leader's goal is to develop leaders, not followers. Although teaching skills is important, the real goal is to develop better people. When that happens God brings out the best because everyone is in sync with God, and seeking to do God's will.

Christian leaders are inspirational by their very nature. It is just who they are – or better said, whose they are. They are servant leaders inspired by Jesus Christ. Others want to be like their caring, Christian leader.

Christian leaders believe in the power of the Trinity. They pray to God, the Father. They follow the example of Jesus Christ, the Son, whose ministry is explained through the scriptures. And they listen for guidance from the Holy Spirit, who places in our hearts and minds the direction to take. Employees will see the peace that faith brings to the leader, and they will want it too.

Leadership style is critical. Hard driving, authoritarian, unforgiving leaders yield unstable staff and volunteers – who are followers and doing only what is asked. Mere employees show little personal commitment because people are afraid of making a mistake. Laissez-faire leaders, in effect, ignore others, leaving them to sink or swim on their own. Laissez-faire leaders have blinders on to the needs of others, and miss the boat on how to develop other people. Contrast those two styles with a Christian leader's style. Christians know who the real leader is. The real leader is Jesus Christ, and not themselves. Jesus Christ empowers people when He said, *You may ask me for anything in my name, and I will do it (John 14:14)*. Because of Jesus' power, the Christian leader will bring success to those they serve.

Question: What characteristics of a Christian leader do you have? What areas are you seeking to improve?

Scripture: *When he had finished washing their feet, he put on his*

25

clothes and returned to his place. "Do you understand what I have done for you?" he asked them. "You call me 'Teacher' and 'Lord,' and rightly so, for that is what I am. Now that I, your Lord and Teacher, have washed your feet, you also should wash one another's feet. I have set you an example that you should do as I have done for you. Very truly I tell you, no servant is greater than his master, nor is a messenger greater than the one who sent him" (John 13:12-16).

Prayer: Dear Lord, we thank You for Christian leaders you have placed in our midst. Even better, You have given us the example of a leader in Jesus Christ. Help us develop our own leadership style that is in keeping with the perfect example of Jesus Christ. Amen.

Topic: Compromising Our Values

Compromise

Spiritual death happens one compromise at a time

Lawmakers do it frequently. They often come to an agreement with people of opposing opinions to "give a little to gain a little." In order to get what they want they say, "If you support my bill I'll support yours." In a word – compromise. Compromises are negotiated agreements. Your goal is to get what you want, knowing at the same time, you are also supporting something you actually don't agree with.

The dictionary gives three meanings of the word: (1) a way of reaching an agreement in which each person or group gives up something that was wanted, in order to end an argument or dispute; (2) something that combines the qualities of two different things; and (3) a change that makes something *worse* and is not done for a good reason.

Nowhere in the definition is there consideration of what is actually the "right thing to do." It is all about settling an argument even if making something worse: it is not doing the right thing at all.

The Bible clearly tells us what the right thing to do is. The argument comes into play when we don't *want* to do what is right, and we try to justify our position. As soon as we start to justify our actions, we know in our hearts we are going against God's will. What we give up is our relationship with God because we want God to give in. As loving as Jesus Christ is, He never gives in to sinful choices. Yes, He forgives our sins. Our part of seeking forgiveness is to pledge not to do it again. Jesus looks into our heart to see if we are sincere, or merely are bargaining to get what we want.

Each time we give in to intentional sin we widen the gap between ourselves and God. Jesus said, *If you love me, keep my commands (John 14:15).* There is no question of His love for us, but how much do *we* love Jesus? When we compromise our beliefs, we are placing ourselves first, above God.

We do have a roadmap, so there is no question of what is the right thing to do. The Bible clearly gives us the direction we should follow. And God does not negotiate. *If anyone, then, knows the good they ought to do and doesn't do it, it is sin for them (James 4:17).*

Remember the legislators who have the authority to create the law of the land. Without them our secular world would be chaotic. God makes the laws that govern our hearts. Without His direction our lives would be confusing and chaotic as well. *Everyone who sins breaks the law; in fact, sin is lawlessness (1 John 3:4).*

So, don't compromise your beliefs. Don't give in. What is right is not negotiable. Each time you try to make your own rules, you move further away from your loving Father.

Question: How do you avoid compromising your values to do the right thing?

Prayer: Heavenly Father, we thank You for taking away the uncertainty of what is right and wrong. We pray we will draw upon You for strength to overcome the temptation to make bad choices. Amen.

Topic: Consistency of God

Characters for the Ages

Disney World is a place many people visit more than once in their lives. Although there have been new additions to the attractions over the years, Mickey, Minnie, Donald Duck, Peter Pan, Cinderella and the other characters are still the stars in the Magic Kingdom. Who can forget the ageless tune, "It's a Small World," and Epcot's familiar Figment, singing his theme song, "Imagination?" Visiting each of the four Disney theme parks, I get the impression that time has stood still. We're still back in the 1970's.

For parents, the Disney characters depict the wholesome, simplistic values of our youth. Disney cartoons always showed good triumphing over evil. We knew the good guys were going to win over any challenge, so we didn't need to take the dangerous characters too seriously. As a result, the world was seen as a happy place. When Walt Disney opened the Magic Kingdom in 1971 he wanted

Disney World to be a place of "joy and inspiration to all who come to this happy place."

Wouldn't it be great if we could go back to the good old days of our youth? It would be like establishing permanent residence at Disney World. Life would be simple and more wholesome, and the end result would be a victory for the good guys. Every generation thinks their good old days were the best ever, regardless if it is set in the 1920's, 1940's, 1960's or even the 1990's. Today's world is more complicated; it seems more difficult to determine right from wrong. Our world *is* more complicated, but right and wrong has never changed. What changes over time is the setting where we live out our moral character.

Simple and wholesome values are the same today as they were when Moses brought the two tablets down from Mt. Sinai. There

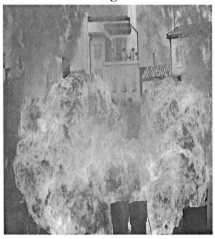

is no evolution of right and wrong. *Jesus Christ is the same yesterday and today and forever (Hebrews 13:8).* Our world changes constantly, but what is right never does.

Imagine yourself on a high-speed Disney ride with the whole world crumbling around you, but your transport vehicle stays on the path to truth and righteousness as it carries you to safety. Behind, you see a scene of destruction and devastation, but you made it through. There are dangers ahead of you, but you know God will take care of you. Good does triumph over evil – in the happy world of Disney and in our everyday world where we live if we let God be at the controls.

People tremble when Captain Hook appears, but he goes into panic mode himself at the sound of a ticking clock. God can bring you through times of trouble and into safety. You can count on

God to be as ageless and loving as the historic Disney characters, providing joy, inspiration and comfort to help you rise above the crumbling world where we live.

Scripture: *God will yet fill your mouth with laughter and your lips with shouts of joy (Job 8:21).*

Question: Do we allow the changing culture around us to affect what we consider to be right and wrong?

Prayer   Heavenly Father, we live in a changing, challenging world. What doesn't change, Lord, is your loving commandments for how we are to lead our lives. Help us as we show others how to live a life of righteousness and joy in a chaotic world. Amen.

Bruce Boyer

Topic: Creation

All We Can Do Is Marvel

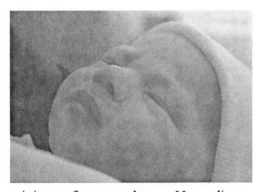 On Friday, May 29, Abigail Leigh Boyer made her grand appearance into our world. Her 11:14 PM birth brought smiles and tears of joy to many people. Such a precious child, she made the wait worthwhile. Abigail had 10 miniature fingers and toes. Her radiant eyes gleamed a bright blue, and thin blond hair capped her head. She sneezed and yawned. She fed on natural milk and she took comfort in being held by loving family members.

So how does a baby minutes into life outside the womb know how to do all these things? The simple answer is Abigail is an intricate creation of God. All the systems of the her tiny body are put exactly where they need to be for her to breathe, for the heart to beat, and for her mind to begin to process information. Very quickly Abigail will realize the specialness of her parents' love for her, and she will return that love. After all, God is love.

As grandparents we can only marvel at God's creation. Shortly after birth we held in our arms a beautiful, perfectly designed little girl. *So God created mankind in his own image, in the image of God he created them; male and female he created them (Genesis 1:27).*

Even though our relationship with Abigail started at 11:14 that evening, God's work started much earlier. Years ago He created Abbie's parents and carefully placed them on paths that would intersect. Their love for each other is the human part of the creation process. God created Abigail's entire line of ancestry with her in mind. His plans stretch from the beginning to the end of time with each person created for a purpose. We look forward to finding out His purpose for Abigail just as He has a purpose for you, too.

Abigail is a beautiful young lady. It will take years to determine her purpose in life. Meanwhile, let us just marvel at God's handiwork. It is special! *God saw all that he had made, and it was very good (Genesis 1:31).*

Scripture: *Before I formed you in the womb I knew you, before you were born I set you apart; I appointed you as a prophet to the nations (Jeremiah 1:5).*

Question: How do you see God at work in the birth of a new child of God?

Prayer: Dear Lord, we thank You for new life. You bring into the world a little bundle of joy which reminds us of Your love for each of us. You have created each of us for a purpose. Let us appreciate the life You have given us and the opportunity to live with purpose. Amen.

Topic: Decisions

My Will or Thy Will?

Conference and NCAA basketball tournaments bring out another side of our personality. Parochialism towards our favorite team intensifies to the point that we no longer are objective. We want every call in favor of our team, regardless if it is right or not. Like the old Burger King commercial, we want to have it our way. The stakes are high, as teams try to qualify for a good seed in the NCAA tournament.

People also have a mind of their own when it comes to making key decisions. They set their mind on something and block out reality. It is all about getting their way regardless of what is right. They want to be in control regardless.

The most popular prayer in the world is The Lord's Prayer. It is regarded as the perfect prayer, taught by Jesus Christ as part of The Sermon on the Mount *(Matthew 6:9-13)*. Nearly everyone who has ever set foot in a church knows it from memory. Notice, I didn't say "by heart." By heart infers that we believe it wholeheartedly so much that we will follow it unconditionally.

Why am I so hard on questioning whether people really believe what they say when they recite The Lord's Prayer? Unfortunately, we conveniently overlook or minimize portions of the prayer to fit our own desires. We readily know the phrase, *Thy will be done*, but often downplay the next line, *on earth as it is in Heaven*. Thy Will is OK when we refer to the abstract of God's home court, Heaven. Our own home court, however, is earth, where we resist giving up control. It is OK when God's Will matches our own, but when it doesn't, we'll hold on for dear life for what we want. With white knuckles and two hands forming a death grip, we'll often keep insisting our way is the only way. We don't want to listen for or accept God's Will.

On the basketball court, coaches display angry behavior when things don't go their way. If a close call goes against them they vehemently protest in hopes of getting the next call. It's called gamesmanship, which is an attempt to be in control. As a fan we are powerless to control the game so we hope video replays will justify our biased opinions.

If we ask for the Lord's guidance we can rest assured that God's call is right every time. God has something much better than instant replay. God has the benefit of knowing what will happen in the future. His vision is for long term gain, so if we follow God's Will, good will happen.

There are all kinds of situations where we don't want to listen for God's will that may differ from our own: a loved one or friend is sick and in great pain. Our agenda is for the person to live regardless of what that means for the person. A job is going badly and we are afraid to look for another in spite of the stress it is causing us. We don't want to face up to a situation because our will might be in conflict with God's will. Who do you think knows what is best in the long run, you or God? Do you really trust God with your life?

Pray to understand God's Will, and trust that it is better than our own tunnel vision. In the game of life, accept God's Will and it will lead you to a triumph: a place on the victory stand called Heaven. Assured of victory, you can cut down the net as you enter the biggest dance imaginable -- Heaven.

Scripture: *This is what the* LORD *says—your Redeemer, the Holy One of Israel: "I am the* LORD *your God, who teaches you what is best for you, who directs you in the way you should go" (Isaiah 48:17).*

Question: What do you do to determine God's will for situations in your life, and how do you act if His Will is different than your own desires?

Prayer: Dear Lord, we tend to want things our way, often without regard for what is right in the long run. Help us to seek and follow Your Will when we make key decisions in life. We trust You with our lives. In Jesus' name we pray. Amen.

Topic: Empowering the
Less Fortunate to Achieve

The Shoe Shine Boy

 As the businessman left the church he was greeted by a host of small children peddling their wares and services. That is the norm in underdeveloped countries like Ecuador, where children regularly sell candy and flowers or perform services to support their families. The kind, church-going businessman agreed to let an 8-year boy shine his shoes. The asking price was 25 cents, but in his mind, the businessman thought he would pay the youngster double. It was to be his good deed for the day. Then the thought came to him, "I wonder if the boy is hungry." The boy said he was hungry, so the businessman took Juan to a nearby bakery for bread and yogurt. They talked as the boy quickly consumed his meal. Oscar asked Juan if he would like to go to a church service. Juan readily agreed, and after the service, he asked Oscar about the book in his hand. "It is my Bible" said Oscar. "Would you like a children's Bible of

your own?" Juan immediately said "yes" so they made plans to meet for breakfast and church the following week. That next week not only did Juan show up, so did three other boys.

Our temptation is to give money to people in need and think we are doing a good deed. While it may feed someone for the moment, it can cause dependence on handouts to sustain their way of life. Juan needed a *relationship* with someone who cared, and who could help the boy start a relationship with God. Realizing the need was much more than a 25 cent shoeshine, the relationship became the catalyst for the Pan de Vida ministry in Quito, Ecuador. Pan de Vida would become a ministry that empowers the poor through job skills training, medical care, learning about Christ, as well as providing food, clothing and school supplies. The name Pan de Vida means "bread of life." Jesus *is* the bread of life, and people with Christ in their life will never go hungry. Instead of being an enabler of dependency, the ministry helps improve a person's self-esteem and self-worth, and to become independent. For example, graduates of the sewing job training program receive a sewing machine of their own. Then they will have the capability to make clothes for their family and sell articles they make to support their family. That is quite different than just handing a person money and thinking we have done a good deed.

Mission teams visiting Pan de Vida have established personal relationships with the beneficiaries there. A local church mission team member purchased a computer for a young man she met in Ecuador. Now, the young man is studying accounting in college – quite a change from selling candy in the streets. Contributions from the same church paid for a surgery that saved the life of a mother in Ecuador. She now is back at work and supporting her family. Money given to the ministry is invested in people to help them rise above their situations. As people graduate from the program they can now turn their attention to the next person in need. Graduates often return as volunteers to help others.

"Poverty is a state of heart and mind," said Oscar Aguirre. "People are impoverished if they don't have love and hope in their lives."

As you look for ways to best utilize your charitable support, look for causes that empower people to develop a career, to be able to work in support of their family, or to improve their health. Seek causes that create an environment of hope. Look for faith-based ministries that combine the strength of many to accomplish great purposes. We don't need to be heroes; we already have a hero in Jesus Christ. Be in partnership with Jesus Christ, follow his lead, and help others to have a future.

The ministry all started when God placed an 8-year old boy in the path of a man with a heart for helping people. Instead of shining shoes to feed his family for a day, the new relationship with Oscar created a ministry to help people for a lifetime.

Question: Which would make you feel better, giving food for a day or hope for the future, and why?

Scripture: *Then Jesus declared, 'I am the bread of life. Whoever comes to me will never go hungry, and whoever believes in me will never be thirsty' (John 6:35).*

Prayer: Heavenly Father, there are many people with needs in this world. We realize, Lord, that the best way we can help others is to share Your love with everyone, but to do it in a way that helps them to grow in their own self-worth and faith in You. Amen.

Bruce Boyer

Topic: Empowered for
Mission & Service

Being Clark Kent Is
Only My Day Job

 Faster than a speeding bullet!
More powerful than a locomo-
tive! Able to leap tall buildings
in a single bound! "Look! Up
in the sky!" "It's a bird!" "It's a
plane!" "It's Superman!" Yes,
it's Superman... strange visitor
from another planet, who came
to Earth with powers and abili-
ties far beyond those of mortal men! Superman... who can change
the course of mighty rivers, bend steel in his bare hands, and who,
disguised as Clark Kent, mild-mannered reporter for a great met-
ropolitan newspaper, fights a never-ending battle for truth, justice,
and the American way!

-- Introduction from the Original TV Show:

The fictional character Clark Kent wears glasses, stumbles frequently, and seems out of place socially. Clark Kent acts insecure, but we all know there is much more to the character than meets the eye. When a crisis hits, Clark Kent seems to disappear. Behind the scenes he transforms himself into Superman, red cape and all. He flies off to the disaster as on a mission, with great strength, confidence, and commitment. Other than the TV viewers, fellow characters in the show never make the connection that mild-mannered Clark Kent and Superman are the same person. His hidden identity allows him to live a normal life but do extraordinary things.

You have that same opportunity to live a normal life but do extraordinary things. Few of us get to work for a mission organization but we all have the opportunity to be mission-driven. We can work our day job as electricians, janitors, sales people, or whatever, but still have another dimension that is mission-oriented. We don't have to save the world, but we can help people according to their needs. Your mission might be to care for an aging parent or elderly neighbor next door. You might be the Christian friend when someone needs guidance. You might be a Sunday School teacher or volunteer with organizations like the Shepherds Center, Crisis Control, or the YMCA. You might participate in domestic or international mission programs with your church. You may be a person who makes the coffee each Sunday morning at church or picks up litter in the parking lot. It doesn't matter how public or private your service is; if it is for the Lord, it is important.

Clark Kent's superhuman powers are with him even when he is in his reporter mode for the <u>Daily Planet</u>. His superhuman sight and hearing detected situations that needed his attention. The same is true for us on our day jobs. We can care for others and be an inspiration for others in the workplace and in our families. We can be superhuman too, when empowered by the Holy Spirit. God gives you the words to say when encouraging others in the faith. You don't need a divinity degree to tell others of Jesus' love. You just have to keep Jesus in your heart.

In the vintage TV series the announcer says that Superman "Came to Earth with powers and abilities far beyond those of mortal men." That is minuscule compared to the powers with which Jesus came to earth. He empowers us as we serve others in His name. The show's introduction continues to say that Superman "Fights a never-ending battle for truth, justice, and the American way!" This world is fighting a never-ending battle to serve needs, but God's empowering love is never-ending too.

Superman accomplishes much with superhuman strength in his make-believe world. Jesus does far more with just love and compassion in the real world. If you have Jesus' love and compassion you have powers and abilities that far exceed those of men without faith. You don't have to change into your tights and red cape, and jump out windows to save the world. Jesus does the saving. Your mission can be just to share His love.

Scripture: *But you shall receive power when the Holy Spirit has come upon you; and you shall be my witnesses in Jerusalem and in all Judea and Samaria and to the end of the earth (Acts 1:8).*

Question: How are you serving God? Do you feel God empowers you to do more than you could on your own?

Prayer: Heavenly Father, we thank You for the skills and abilities You gave us, allowing us to support our families, but also equipping us help others. There is only one fictional Superman, but there are many of us willing to serve You by serving others. Amen.

Topic: Eternal Gift

Our Next Millionaire

I watched the show "The Millionaire" on black and white television back when I was in grade school. The idea behind the 1950's television show was to see how unexpected wealth changed lives for better or for worse. The $1 million check came as a surprise, given by an anonymous benefactor who insisted people never know his identity. My favorite line in each show is when the benefactor says, "Our next millionaire," as he gives the check to the messenger who would present it to the lucky recipient.

My eyes would always focus on the check as he was handing it off. In my mind I always wondered how a check like that would change things for me.

In the 1950's $1 million was an astronomical, life-changing

amount. At that time even professional athletes and movie stars never earned that kind of income. The recipient's life was never the same after that: sometimes for the better, but sometimes with opposite results.

What would you do with $1 million? You could buy the yacht or vacation home of your dreams. You could invest it, pay off loans, take care of your parents, or do things for your kids. You could now seemingly do anything you wanted. What a life-changing gift $1 million would be.

Picture yourself as the benefactor, giving the gift to a family member or, in the case of the television program, a perfect stranger. You know you are enabling a new perspective on life. As substantial as the amount is, in the grand scheme of things, the gift is short-lived.

By contrast, what if you were able to give a gift that lasts *forever?* Wouldn't that be a better gift? What if they also passed on that eternal gift to others, multiplying the effect of your single gift? The value of your eternal gift is far greater than the principle and compounding interest of $1 million, even if invested since the days of black and white TV. You couldn't put a price tag on that kind of gift. A $1 million gift would be miniscule compared to an eternal gift.

The most valuable gift you can ever give someone is the gift of faith. You can change a life forever if you share God's plan for salvation with someone who has not received it. If they accept Jesus Christ as their Lord and Savior, they are on the way to heaven – forever. Actuarial tables can be tossed aside. Your gift is forever, and undoubtedly life-changing. There is nothing better you can do for someone.

It takes us stepping out of our comfort zone and perhaps risking a little as we encourage people to attend church, and find ways to nurture their faith. But, what a difference it will make in their lives. The thanks you receive will be seeing that person every day for eternity, with the knowledge the Holy Spirit worked through you to encourage their relationship with God. You plant the seed and God does the rest. Then you can say my favorite line, "Our next millionaire."

Scripture: *For if you confess with your mouth that Jesus is Lord and believe in your heart that God raised him from the dead, you will be saved. For it is by believing in your heart that you are made right with God, and it is by confessing with your mouth that you are saved. As the Scriptures tell us, 'Anyone who believes in him will not be disappointed' (Romans 10:9-11).*

Question: How would your life be different if you were given $1 million?

Prayer: Dear Lord, our world places currency as the ultimate goal. Help us to understand that the gift of faith is far more important than the gift of money. Help us to share our faith with others. Amen.

Bruce Boyer

Living the Faith

The light turned yellow, just in front of him. The driver did the right thing and stopped at the crosswalk, resisting the urge to accelerate through the intersection.

The tailgaiting woman behind him was furious and honked her horn, screaming in frustration as she missed her chance to hurry through the intersection – on a red light. As the tailgater was still in mid-rant, she heard a tap on her window and looked into the serious face of a police officer. The officer ordered her to exit her car with her hands up. He took her to the police station where she was searched, fingerprinted, photographed and placed in a holding cell.

After a couple of hours, a policeman approached the cell and opened the door. The tailgating driver was escorted back to the booking desk where the arresting officer was waiting with her personal effects.

The policeman said, "I'm very sorry for this mistake. You see, I pulled up behind your car while you were blowing your horn, giving the guy in front of you the finger and cursing at him. I noticed the 'What Would Jesus Do' bumper sticker, the 'Choose Life' license plate holder, the 'Follow Me to Sunday School' bumper sticker, and the chrome-plated Christian fish emblem on the trunk. Naturally, I assumed you had stolen the car."

This is not an original story, but copied from a Facebook post. It may be an exaggeration, but it gives a very clear message. People who see your symbols of faith anticipate you will live accoringly. Our faith speaks of compassion, forgiveness, and caring about other people. When we act contrary to our faith, it bursts a big bubble and the believability of what our faith teaches us.

Consider these revealing questions:

- Do we advertise we are a Christian but act otherwise?
- Are the bumper stickers, crosses on our necklasses, and the display of Christian symbols just an act?
- Are we trying to impress people with our pious appearance, but are really something different in real life?
- Is our Christian faith something to feel good about during the good times, but we throw it out the window when times get tough?

It is great to promote our faith by displaying Christian symbols. Our objective is for people to see us living a life of peace and grace, knowing we are Christian, and want to also experience the hope we have in Jesus Christ. However, when we identify ourselves as Christians but act just the opposite, we do a disservice to the faith. *Whoever says, "I know him" but does not do what he commands is a liar, and the truth is not in that person (1 John 2:4).*

The stronger the statement we make about being a Christian, the bigger a target we are to Satan. Satan will place lots of red lights in our paths to test us. People who have rejected the faith look for opportunities to chastise Christians who act as if they don't have

Jesus in their hearts. They love to mock hyporocrits, as it justifies their position that faith doesn't make a difference.

Let your faith bring you peace in the face of adversity. And let your actions match the "What Would Jesus Do" sticker.

Scripture: *Let your light shine before men, that they may see your good works and give glory to your Father who is in heaven (Matthew 5:16).*

Prayer: Lord, we thank you for showing us how to live our lives. We pray we will tell others about you and then do our best of live a life in keeping with your teachings. Amen.

Topic: Faith Like a Child

Receiving the Kingdom Like a Child

The one-year-old boy was into everything. With youthful enthusiasm he explored his world, pulling toys off the shelf and crawling up and down the hall, laughing all the way. He was curious how things worked, pushing all the buttons on his electronic toys. He giggled when he thought he was doing something special or in response to others. Even though he wasn't walking yet, that didn't stop him from getting to where he wanted to go. He could stand holding onto things and if he fell down, he would get right back up and try again. Put things up high and the youngster would try to find a way, any way, to reach the object of his fascination.

At the baptism the pastor read the familiar scripture verse: Jesus said, *Truly I tell you, unless you change and become like little children, you will never enter the kingdom of heaven (Matthew 18:3).*

Looking at our smiling, happy grandson, the Bible verse made sense. Adults set up arbitrary boundaries that limit their achievement. Adults are preoccupied with the enormity of life and look for reasons to avoid investing themselves fully in deepening their faith. In contrast, a child has no boundaries. He just wants to explore and learn. When Jesus said, *Truly I tell you, anyone who will not receive the kingdom of God like a little child will never enter it (Luke 18:17)*, it made perfect sense. A youthful zeal and an eagerness to learn is the key to a true relationship with Jesus.

The world of a one-year-old is fueled by the bond of love for family, with a dependency to provide daily nourishment. We can learn from a child if we let down our resistance and allow Jesus Christ into our lives to nourish our souls.

Our faith can be strengthened with the unbridled enthusiasm of a youngster, eager to explore and to learn. That's what God wants us to do. Don't let obstacles or complicated agendas deter you from seeking a pure, loving relationship with Jesus Christ.

Scripture: *Let the little children come to me, and do not hinder them, for the kingdom of God belongs to such as these. Truly I tell you, anyone who will not receive the kingdom of God like a little child will never enter it (Mark 10:14-15).*

Question: Can you put aside the tendency to be so carefully guarded, only letting Jesus impact a small part of your life? How can you show youthful enthusiasm for your faith?

Prayer: Dear Lord, help us to let down our guard and let You more fully into our lives. Help us to overcome the obstacles we place in our own path and seek You with our whole heart. Amen.

Topic: Fear

Fear Not

Many people live a life of fear. Some are afraid of animate objects, such as snakes, spiders, birds, or large wild animals. For others, their deepest fear is failure. Children often fear the dark because of unknown or imagined dangers lurking under their bed or in their closet. Some people fear dying, also because of the unknown. Fear of rejection causes us to freeze in our tracks and do nothing.

People are afraid to act and instead, ball up in an imaginary fetal position. They hope whatever is the cause of their fear will pass them by, the sun will rise, and everything will be okay. But nothing happened and nothing changed. We failed *because* we didn't act. A person afraid of being rejected when sharing their faith didn't even have a chance to win a soul for Christ; instead, he kept his faith to himself.

There certainly are unknowns in our daily lives. What is about to happen is only unknown to us. God knows exactly what is in store for us. If you fix your eyes on your own naval in the fetal position you are letting your own humanity block the potential for real gain. When you fix your eyes on Jesus, the potential is unlimited. Fear is a lack of faith that God is in control and will take care of you.

Remember the disciples in the boat, seeing a man walking on the water towards them. Walking on water is impossible without God. The disciples were afraid, thinking they were seeing a ghost. *Take courage! It is I. Don't be afraid, Jesus said (Mark 6:50).* Remember Peter asking Jesus to allow him to also walk on the water. As long as Peter's eyes were fixed on Jesus, he walked on water. When Peter began to doubt, he instantly started to sink. *Let us fix our eyes on Jesus, the author and perfecter of our faith (Hebrews 12:2).* We can do the miraculous if we fix our eyes on Jesus and trust him to help us do the extraordinary.

Don't let your comfort zone become your coffin of inactivity. God protected Paul in Corinth. *For I am with you, and no one is going to attack and harm you, because I have many people in this city (Acts 18:10).* Even in human conflict the Lord calms the fears of Gideon and Joshua when he says, *Peace! Do not be afraid. You are not going to die (Judges 6:23).*

How does he do this? God empowers the faithful. Without God's power you are restricted to human limitations. Mary was afraid when the angels approached her, telling her she would bear a child named Jesus. *Do not be afraid, Mary, you have found favor with God (Luke 1:30).* She mothered the Savior of the World. With God, anything is possible. He chose you to doing something significant for Him.

You are not alone. Fear is the most commonly used word in the

Bible. We all have our fears. But, the Bible accompanies the use of the word fear with the assurance that God is with us. I wouldn't step on a snake or jump off a cliff without a parachute, but I would trust that God gives me wisdom to make good choices in life and the understanding He will be with me when my choices are made to glorify God.

Question: What fears do you have that prevent you from taking action?

Prayer: Lord, we all have fears – some real and some imaginary. Help us to overcome the fears that would otherwise hold us back from being the person you created us to be. We pray our comfort zone will be the comfort You give us. Be with us always, to the end of the age. Amen.

Topic: Forgiveness

Avoiding the Issue

When I was in college a good friend of mine asked to borrow $50. He had a very pressing need, and I was more than willing to help. My friend said he would pay it back the first of the next month. The first of next month came and went and my friend was nowhere to be seen. He not only didn't pay back the $50 but it seemed that he was avoiding me. He didn't come around to my dorm room, and I never saw him in the cafeteria. On several occasions I could see him coming down the hall toward me, but suddenly he would change directions. It seemed when he saw me he would go another direction, always avoiding me. What had I done to deserve this treatment?

As luck would have it I finally cornered him and asked him why he was avoiding me. He explained that he was embarrassed because couldn't pay back the $50. He was avoiding me because he didn't want to admit he couldn't pay his friend back. In effect, he was distancing himself from me.

By avoiding me, he took away my opportunity to forgive his debt. I would have helped. What are friends for? Because he didn't ask for help I couldn't forgive his debt. If I hadn't cornered him he might have awkwardly avoided me forever.

When something goes wrong for us, do we avoid asking God for forgiveness? Do we hide from the Lord? Do we take away the Lord's opportunity to forgive because we avoid asking? Are we ducking the issue because we are embarrassed?

I would have forgiven my friend, and in my time of need, undoubtedly, the Lord would have forgiven me. But we have to ask.

Don't underestimate the Lord's capacity to forgive. Forgiveness is one of His greatest gifts, and it allows us to live in peace and joy. All we have to do is ask.

Scripture: *For if you forgive men their trespasses, your heavenly Father will also forgive you. But, if you do not forgive men their trespasses, neither will your Father forgive your trespasses (Matthew 6:14-15).*

Question: Do you hesitate to ask God for His forgiveness, because you are embarrassed?

Prayer: Dear Lord, we are in need of forgiveness. Please keep us humble so that we will be willing to ask You for forgiveness. And let us be eager to forgive others. Amen.

Bruce Boyer

Topic: Glorifying God

Who Is #1?

 T-shirts say a lot about people. You can tell what sports team people cheer for by the apparel they wear. You can identify a favorite vacation spot by the logo on someone's clothing. Shirts state a philosophy of life such as "Life is a Beach" or "I Put the Pro in Procrastination." I like to wear shirts that display the theme of YMCA Christian Leadership Conferences because they speak about leadership from a Christian perspective. These are the messages I want to portray.

One shirt I saw recently out in the community said, "It's All About Me," with ME in very large letters. Like many t-shirt statements you can interpret it many ways. An egotistical person may be making a statement about their priority in life being themselves. Who is #1? But change the last word from Me to Him – with a capital "H" and it takes on an entirely different meaning. It puts our focus on God and not self. Everything we do should be to glorify Him. *So whether you eat or drink or whatever you do, do it all for the glory of God (1 Corinthians 10:31).* Let your words and actions show that your life is all about God.

Our life is dramatically different if we are all about glorifying God, and not serving ourselves. When you dedicate your life to Christ the verse from Galatians 2:20 sums it up well: *I have been crucified with Christ and I no longer live, but Christ lives in me. The life I now live in the body, I live by faith in the Son of God, who loved me and gave himself for me.*

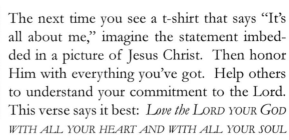

The next time you see a t-shirt that says "It's all about me," imagine the statement imbedded in a picture of Jesus Christ. Then honor Him with everything you've got. Help others to understand your commitment to the Lord. This verse says it best: *Love the Lord your God with all your heart and with all your soul and with all your strength (Deuteronomy 6:5).*

Question: In what ways can you glorify God through your daily life?

Prayer: Heavenly Father, all that we have comes from You. You are the light that guides our path, comforts and strengthens us when things are difficult, and gives us assurance of the life to come. Lord, let our life be all about You. We pray others will see these qualities and also want to live their lives for You. Amen.

Bruce Boyer

Topic: God Knows
You Intimately

How Does He Do That?

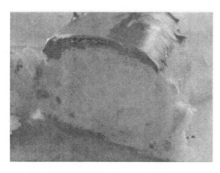

I got caught red-handed on the night before Valentine's Day. I occasionally shopped at a business named Intown Donutz. My typical order is a single doughnut – chocolate-covered and cream-filled. The owner of the shop, a young lady named Teany, greets me by name each time I am there. In fact, my second time in the store "T" greeted me by name. The plot thickened when my wife visited Intown Dountz to buy doughnuts to celebrate Valentine's Day. When Kathy arrived at the doughnut shop "T" asked who she was. Kathy identified herself as Kathy Boyer. My cover was blown when the shop owner immediately said, "Oh, Bruce was just in here this morning." Busted!

A month later I went in for a doughnut and "T" asked me, "How is Kathy?" She met Kathy one time a month ago and still remembered her name. What amazing customer service! Calling anyone by name makes them feel welcome.

That brings to mind the question, how does God know our name? As the creator of the universe with an astronomically large number of people who have lived on this earth, how does He remember who we are? Like "T", God not only knows every name but the connections we have with our family, our friends, and our needs. He knows what issues we face. The Bible says, *And even the very hairs of your head are all numbered (Matthew 10:30).* For some of us, that is a small number. But it is all part of God being invested in us.

A simple answer to the rhetorical question is that He knows everyone because He is God. And he cares. He cares about you and the people connected to you. He has plans for you. Don't ever underestimate God's power and his caring. As Christians we know of God's sacrifice of his Son, Jesus Christ, so we can have everlasting life in a heavenly environment where the doughnuts are fresh and are our favorite kind. He knows us intimately. He cares. He loves. And He is God.

Scripture: *Jesus said, "The Father himself loves you because you have loved me and have believed that I came from God" (John 16:27).*

Question: How much about you do you think God knows?

Prayer: We thank you, Lord, for knowing all about us. You know what we need. Let us listen to You as You guide our lives. Amen.

Bruce Boyer

Topic: God's Unlimited Power

Achieving the Unachievable

The 2015-16 NBA season experienced a historic moment. On the last day of the regular season the Golden State Warriors had a chance to win a record 73 wins. Their coach, Steve Kerr, had played for the Chicago Bulls which set the seemingly unbeatable record of 72 wins. As a member of the Bulls, he thought there was no way any team would ever top their mark. Then he coached the team who did just that. In such a highly competitive sport as professional basketball, winning 73 of 82 games is amazing. But it wasn't impossible. In the same game Warriors guard Steph Curry finished with a record 402 3-point field goals for the season.

As humans we tend to put limitations on what we can accomplish. Just because the previous record took a monumental effort, we think that is as good as it gets. With God's help we can accomplish much more than anyone ever thought possible. That is the meaning of my favorite Bible passage, *Philippians 4:13*, which says *with*

God all things are possible.

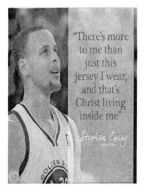

"There's more to me than just this jersey I wear, and that's Christ living inside me"

Stephen Curry

I certainly am not implying the Warriors' success was divinely inspired, but the possibility remains that it may have been part of God's plan. God ensures the success of humans when they are following His plan, even though we may not know it at the time. His plan may be revealed much later. Perhaps Steph Curry and the other players of faith on the Warriors team may utilize their success on the court to win people for Christ.

There is no limit on what God can do. His unlimited potential certainly surpasses all human understanding. We can't even begin to imagine how God spoke the world into existence, creating the heavens and the earth, and everything in between. While impossible by human standards, everything is possible for God. He did it.

Is it possible for a basketball team to win more than 73 games during the regular season? If God wants it to happen, it will. Don't place human limitations on our God who has unlimited power.

How about you? Just think what He could do with your life if you let Him be the source of your strength. *Trust in the* LORD *WITH ALL YOUR HEART, AND DO NOT RELY ON YOUR OWN INSIGHT. IN ALL YOUR WAYS ACKNOWLEDGE HIM, AND HE WILL MAKE STRAIGHT YOUR PATHS* (PROVERBS 3:5-6). Turn your life over to God, and anything can happen.

Question: How do you think God would change your life if you turned your life over to Him?

Scripture: *But Jesus looked at them and said, "With man this is impossible, but with God all things are possible"(Matthew 19:26).*

Bruce Boyer

It is he who made the earth by his power, who established the world by his wisdom, and by his understanding stretched out the heaven (Jeremiah 10:12).

Prayer: Heavenly Father, no task is too big for You. Nothing is impossible. Help us to understand Your plan for our lives, and then give us the confidence to live the plan. Amen.

Topic: Decisions

Consequences

 My computer has a game called Free Cell, a modified game of Solitaire, which allows you to temporarily move 4 cards to the side while you play other cards. Throughout the entire game all 52 cards are on display, so there are no surprises. Sounds simple, doesn't it? Not the way I often play the game.

When I play Free Cell my first instinct is to immediately move the easy cards. I do this without scanning the entire field and planning future moves. I just play what is easy because I can, not because I should. After several hasty moves, I see my options are now limited. Then I study the field. Ignoring the consequences of not evaluating the results of my actions is often a recipe for disaster. I would be far better off creating the plan first before boxing myself into a corner. When I play the easy cards first, I ignore the later consequences of my actions.

In our everyday lives we may do the same thing. Some decisions seem easy and are made quickly, often without thinking. We do something merely because the opportunity is there, regardless of whether it is right or wrong. The truth is, easy decisions are not always the right ones, and may position us for disaster later in life. There are consequences to our actions: a wrong move in Free Cell or a poor choice in life.

Before diving into a task, first ask God for direction. With the wisdom of God's direction you can scan the full field and make the right choice. You certainly can ask yourself, "What would God do?"

It is not important to God if I win at Free Cell, but the decisions made in life are important to Him. Ask God for direction and He will lead you in the right path.

Question: In the past, how have you weighed options against their consequences before making a decision?

Scripture: *For the Lord gives wisdom, and from his mouth come knowledge and understanding (Proverbs 2:6). Then you will understand what is right and just and fair – every good path (Proverbs 2:9).*

Prayer: Lord, it is easy to merely react to situations we face. We pray we will seek Your direction to lead us on the right path for our lives.

Topic: Handling Anger

Four Things You Can Never Recover

We have all heard the saying, "God is the same yesterday, today and tomorrow." We can count on God and His expectations of us to be consistent.

On the other hand, what are you like? Some days do you start your day full of energy and ready to tackle the world? Other days, it takes several cups of coffee before you are ready to settle at your desk and gradually become productive as the caffeine kicks in. Human nature is to be inconsistent.

My goal is to be predictable and loving, and not just reactive.

Part of being predictable is considering what I do or say before I open my mouth or swing into action. I don't want to live hoping people forgive me for saying the wrong thing or doing something I will regret. *My dear brothers and sisters take note of this: Everyone should be quick to listen, slow to speak and slow to become angry (James 1:19).*

One of my favorite devotional stories, The Fence, articulates the message of being careful of what you say, especially in times of anger. Once something is said or done, we can't "wish" the consequences away.

The Fence

There was a little boy with a bad temper. His father gave him a bag of nails and told him that every time he lost his temper to hammer a nail in the back fence. The first day, the boy had driven 37 nails into the fence. Then it gradually dwindled down. The boy discovered it was easier to hold his temper than to drive those nails into the fence. Finally the day came when the boy didn't lose his temper at all. He told his father about it and the father suggested that the boy now pull out one nail for each day that he was able to hold his temper. The days passed and the young boy was finally able to tell his father that all the nails were gone. The father took his son by the hand and led him to the fence. He said, "You have done well, my son, but look at the holes in the fence. The fence will never be the same. When you say things in anger they leave a scar just like this one. You can put a knife in a man and draw it out. It won't matter how many times you say I'm sorry, the wound is still there."

Four Things You Can Never Recover:
The stone...........after the throw.
The word...........after it is said.
The time...........after it has passed.
The occasion......after it is missed.

Consider what you do or say before you act. Don't miss the opportunity to do something nice instead of saying something in anger you will later regret. Don't miss the opportunity to share your love with someone. Say a kind word to someone every chance you get because you may never get the opportunity again. Hold the negative thought because you also may never get the opportunity to correct it. You only get one chance at this life. Make the best of it. (Fence story author unknown)

Scripture: *Stop being angry! Turn from your rage! Do not lose your temper – it only leads to harm (Psalm 37:8).*

Question: What techniques do you use to not over-react or say something you might regret?

Prayer: Dear Lord, it is easy to forget we are Your disciples and followers, and then react in fallible, human ways to negative situations. Help us to hold our temper and our negative thoughts. Let us always speak and act in love. Amen.

Bruce Boyer

Topic: Honesty and
Respect

... And I Approve This Message

 Each fall "And I approve this mes-
sage" becomes an all-too-familiar
statement on television or the ra-
dio. It is required on all political ads,
proof a candidate agrees with the
content of the ad. Watching some
of the ads, it is a wonder a candi-
date would want to have their name associated with it. The more
contested the race, the nastier the ads have become. Political candidates often spend more effort attacking each other than offering
their own solutions to community problems. Candidates sometimes hold the most damaging accusation until just before Election Day, minimizing an opponent's opportunity to respond. It is
appalling what a candidate will say when under campaign pressure.
When you are under pressure, what comes out of your mouth?
What are you willing to say about someone else? Are you willing
to tell half-truths to boost your own standing? Do you take things
out of context and exploit them for your own purposes?

The Bible gives us clear guidance on how to deal with people who oppose us. *But I tell you, love your enemies and pray for those who persecute you (Matthew 5:44).* We don't see that often on political television ads or debates. We see candidates blaming others for all the ills of the world. In contrast, the Bible tells us to understand and forgive our enemies.

If you are a person of faith, you can have an entirely different way of handling pressure. You can rely on God for answers. If you let God be in control, He will give you peace. God will help establish a more respectful relationship with those who disagree with you. *When the LORD takes pleasure in anyone's way, he causes their enemies to make peace with them (Proverbs 16:7).*

Sometimes we lose sight of who the enemy is. Satan is enemy #1 of an even more important battle than an election or a disagreement in our lives. It is Satan who causes us to act in a sinful, unloving way. When we resist Satan's evil ways we can act with love and compassion. God will give us strength to overcome obstacles and He will provide the answers. In your own stressful situations, seek God's approval. Imagine how different and convincing it would be to hear this tag line: "This is Jesus Christ, and I approve this message."

Question: When under pressure, how can your words and actions be pleasing to God?

Prayer: Dear Lord, we seek to be pleasing to You in all we do. We pray we will be truthful in what we say and honorable in all that we do. We pray we will seek Your guidance when we are under pressure. Amen.

Bruce Boyer

Topic: Hope, Trust &
Overcoming Fear

Learning from Our Mistakes

The toddler was attempting to do what he has seen grownups do: walk. The proud parents gave their best smiles and most encouraging gestures. After many attempts to stand up, the toddler finally made it to his feet and immediately collapsed to the ground. He quickly rose again, only to make a second crash landing. After several more attempts he took his first step, falling forward on his face. A tear or two later, the child tried again. After many failed attempts the toddler finally walked to the outstretched arms of loving parents. Remarkably, the young child was not afraid of failure, only temporarily deterred by the discomfort of falling to the floor. Learning to walk was more important than the fear of failure. And the child learned from his mistakes.

A pottery instructor tried an experiment in a class. The instructor gave half the class the assignment of creating their *one* most perfect piece of pottery. They could spend the entire semester creating a single masterpiece. Their effort focused on perfecting the shape and design of one vase. The other half the class could spend the semester making as many vases as possible, turning in their best one at the end. Their goal seemed to be quantity production.

At the end of the semester, which group provided the best vase? The quantity group won in a landslide. The vase selected by each student in the quantity group was consistently better than the one masterpiece that students had spent the entire semester on. Why? The quantity group learned from their mistakes. Each attempt allowed the student a chance to improve on previous designs.

What we can learn from the toddler and the pottery class is that it is okay to fail as long as you get up and try again. The child never quit trying to walk, and eventually could become a world class athlete, or perhaps just a Little League player giving his best effort on the field. But they all fell before they walked.

In the popular Bible story about the disciples riding in a boat on the stormy seas, Jesus came walking by – walking on water. After finally recognizing Jesus, Peter asked if he could walk on the water, too. Jesus encouraged him, so Peter stepped out of the boat and began walking on water himself. A few steps later Peter began to realize what was happening, and that he really shouldn't have been able to do what he was doing. Fear took over. Peter looked down at the stormy sea and immediately began to sink. When he set his eyes back on Jesus he resumed his miracle walk.

What is happening in this story? **Hope** got Peter out of the boat, embarking on a journey only possible because of God's power. Peter's **trust** in Jesus held him up. Then **fear** took over, Peter lost his focus, his willingness to keep taking the small steps in faith, and then began to sink. Set your eyes on Jesus and you can accomplish remarkable things.

Life has its succession of storms. If we focus our attention on the storms, we will likely sink. Yet, if we can keep our eyes on Jesus, His strength will carry us through the storms of life. It may take the repeated attempts of the toddler learning to walk, but if we place our hope in Jesus Christ, He will carry us through the storm and back to calmer seas.

Question: When you are facing a difficult task, how do you fix your attention on God's power to prevent the enormity of the task from overwhelming you?

Scripture: *Then Peter got down out of the boat, walked on the water and came toward Jesus. But when he saw the wind, he was afraid and, beginning to sink, cried out, "Lord, save me!" Immediately Jesus reached out his hand and caught him. "You of little faith," he said, "why did you doubt?" And when they climbed into the boat, the wind died down (Matthew 14:29-32).*

Prayer: Dear Lord. Life's tasks are enormous. Let us place our eyes on You and put aside our fear of failure. Then, together, we know we will be successful. Amen.

Acknowledgement: The concept of these examples is taken from John Ortberg's book, <u>If You Want to Walk on Water, You've Got to Get Out of the Boat.</u>

Topic: Jesus' Greatness

Discovering Greatness

My dad passed away recently. Family members gathered together  to begin the task of sorting through personal items and correspondence. There was more to the man than we had ever imagined.

Dad was an accomplished electrical engineer and a brilliant man. He had many US patents and was at the cutting edge of communication technology of his time. Evenings and weekends, he designed and installed telephone and PA systems at YMCAs, churches, school systems, Y camps, and even military bases. We sorted through large piles of blueprint drawings and viewed detailed, meticulous operating instructions for all of his electronic creations. What we saw was simply amazing!

Then we found correspondence he had written about all kinds of family topics. He wasn't afraid to speak up to correct a situation. Not only did he stand up for his children, but he also sought information so he could guide us to be better people. He always sought to do the right thing.

Dad always was there when people needed help, whether at church, with family, or in the community. You don't realize the depth of his service until you dig deeper into his life. Dad had quite a legacy, but he never touted himself. He just did it.

Jesus Christ has the ultimate legacy. His work is well documented thanks to the Bible and other supporting references. Jesus rallied  to help people and then humbly said not to tell others what He had done. Jesus acted perfectly with wisdom, foresight, and compassion. A study of His life and teachings reveals the blueprint of how we should live our lives. And speaking of advocacy for others, He will become your advocate when you meet the Heavenly Father. You can't discover His greatness by merely pretending to understand Jesus. You need to study it fully in the Bible.

The only way to understand my Dad's unbelievable accomplishments is to research the man fully. In the same way, the only way to comprehend the fullness of Jesus' life and ministry is to dig into the Word. Discover His greatness. It is simply amazing!

You can't discover His greatness by merely pretending to understand Jesus. You need to study it fully in the Bible.

Remember what your dad has done for you – as a role model, provider, advocate, and parent. Your dad does this because of his love for you. As we discovered in Dad's personal effects, fathers do much more for their children than we realize. Your Heavenly Father is doing great things for you. God provided a role model, his son Jesus Christ, and then sacrificed Him so you can love and have forgiveness. It was all done in love. Remember that three things will endure: *faith, hope and love. And the greatest is these is love (1 Corinthians 13:13).* Happy Father's Day.

Scripture: *To him who alone does great wonders, for his steadfast love endures forever (Psalm 136:4).*

Question: Is your knowledge of Jesus' life and teachings pretty basic or are you making a sincere effort to dig deeper, to learn about the greatness of Jesus? If you do, you will better understand what He has done in love for you.

Prayer: Heavenly Father, this Father's Day we take time to remember what our earthly dads have done for us. Let us remember what You, as the Heavenly Father, have done for all of us.

Topic: Leadership

12 Ordinary Men

It is easy to marvel at the athletic ability of superstars – people who can do superhuman stunts like dunking the basketball, hitting  a tape measure home run. Being a sports star doesn't make a person a star at life. Read the sports pages and you'll find about the real character of some superhuman athletes. An NBA hall of famer was right when he said he "is not a role model."

Would God have chosen any of those athletic stars for His team of disciples? Probably not. Jesus did not choose the superstars of His time either. None of the disciples came from religious backgrounds, but instead, they came from ordinary professions of their time. Four disciples were commercial fishermen – Simon Peter, Andrew, James and John. Matthew was a tax collector, which was considered a disrespectful way of earning a living. Simon the Zealot and Judas Iscariot were probably political activists. In all respects they were twelve very ordinary men, not superstars. And yet, they succeeded in spreading the Good News and, as a result, changing the world. *Brothers and sisters, think of what you were when you were called. Not many of you were wise by human standards; not many were influential; not many were of noble birth (1 Corinthians 1:26).*

Why did God choose the ordinary to begin the process of convincing the world of such an extraordinary message? Because that is the way He works. He doesn't need those who think they are great to do his work. Instead, He needs people who think God is great! He needs you and me.

Do you consider yourself to be a Superman or Wonder Woman? Many of us would rather fade into the woodwork than to be a spokesperson to the world. Our temptation is to look all around us hoping someone else will take the leadership role. "Certainly not me, Lord. Someone else is more qualified than me."

As one of the greatest leaders of the Old Testament, Moses didn't feel qualified to honor God's requests. Moses pleaded, *Lord, please! Send someone else (Exodus 4:13).* So, could he do the job? Armed with God's power, he raised his shepherd's staff and parted the Red Sea. There are countless stories throughout the Bible of great things being done by ordinary people. We can do great things, too, if we utilize the Lord's power to help us do what we couldn't do on our own.

God loves the humble and he puts His faith in those who trust Him, stepping out of their comfort zones and acting from the heart.

So, if we are not academically qualified or otherwise gifted, how do we accomplish tasks that God wants us to do? If you think you lack the skills to do something, ask the Lord to help you. The process of trusting God's strength instead of your own admitted weakness is the very reason why 12 ordinary men were able to change the world. You can do the same. Ask God to guide and lead you. We can make it a baker's dozen.

Question: How can you get the courage to step out of your comfort zone and respond to God's request to lead? What can you do in your local community?

Scripture*:* *Then I heard the Lord asking, "Whom should I send as a messenger to my people? Who will go for us?" And I said, "Lord, I'll go! Send me" (Isaiah 6:8).*

Prayer: Lord, we pray we will respond to Your call to serve. Give us the courage to accept opportunities to serve and lead. Amen.

Topic: Love

Love in All Relationships

The bride and groom stood at the altar during their wedding. A family member read the familiar scripture verse: *Love is patient, love is kind. It does not envy, it does not boast, it is not proud. It does not dishonor others, it is not self-seeking, it is not easily angered, it keeps no record of wrongs. Love does not delight in evil, but rejoices with the truth. It always protects, always trusts, always hopes, always perseveres (1 Corinthians 13:4-7).* Most of us can recite, or at least paraphrase this beautiful passage that describes a loving relationship.

It may surprise you to know that the writer, Paul, didn't pen these words for a wedding ceremony. He wrote them to the church at Corinth because relationships in that congregation lacked love. Love is not intended to be reserved only for a bride, but for all people we meet, including our enemies. It is a benchmark message for all Christians.

What if we substituted the word "I" for love, and then applied it as a plan of action for all of our interactions with people? Now it would say:

- I am patient.
- I am kind.
- I will not envy, I will not boast, and I will not be proud.
- I will not dishonor others.
- I will not be self-seeking.
- I will not be easily angered.
- I will not keep a record of wrongs.
- I will not delight in evil but rejoice in the truth.
- I will always protect, always trust, always hope and always persevere.

Wouldn't following this plan of action make a difference in the kind of person you are and your relationships with everyone?

What if you intentionally used these words as a guide to how you respond to others, including before every meeting and interaction with others? Everything about you would be changed. Isn't that exactly what Jesus wanted for us – to change us to become Godly people? Jesus came to this earth to change the world. He came to bring love to our relationships. All of them.

Question: Can you refocus your interactions to apply love in all relationships, even with those with whom you disagree?

Scripture: *You have heard that it was said, 'Love your neighbor and hate your enemy.' But I tell you, love your enemies and pray for those who persecute you, that you may be children of your Father in heaven. He causes his sun to rise on the evil and the good, and sends rain on the righteous and the unrighteous. If you love those who love you, what reward will you get? Are not even the tax collectors doing that? And if you greet only your own people, what are you doing more than others? Do not even pagans do that? Be perfect, therefore, as your heavenly Father is perfect (Matthew 5:43-48).*

Prayer: Dear Lord, Jesus came to earth to show us how to love. He loved even those who sought to discredit him and eventually take his earthly life. Yet because of His love for us, He conquered evil and gave us a path to Heaven. Amen.

Bruce Boyer

Topic: Love for People
Different Than Us

Loving Americans

One of my favorite movies is <u>The American President.</u> The movie storyline is about a popular, widowed US President who falls in love with an energetic, committed lobbyist. Less than a year be- fore his re-election attempt the romance brings accusations by his leading political opponent. The opponent accuses the girl-friend of being un-American because she expresses a differ-ent point of view. A key line in the movie comes when the Presi-dent says, "It is amazing when a person says he loves America but can't stand Americans." How about you? Do you love America but can't stand Americans who think differently than you?

We live in a country founded on freedom including the freedom of speech. Our country's founding fathers established the United States of America to be tolerant of differing points of view. Over time our society has become more polarized, especially in the po-litical scene. We tend to judge people if they think differently than us.

The most dramatic scene in the movie is when the President addresses a press conference about his political opponent's accusations. He says, "America is advanced citizenship. You have to want it bad." Speaking directly in response to his opponent, he says, "You want free speech: let's see you acknowledge a man who is going to make your blood boil, who would advocate at the top of his lungs that which you would spend a lifetime opposing at the top of yours." He goes on to say if you claim this country as the "land of the free," then you need to respect what freedom stands for.

People of faith have spent a lifetime learning how God wants us to live our lives. Not everyone believes in our God, but thankfully, living in this country, we all have the right to believe in God. We also have the right to express opposing viewpoints. The opposition doesn't have to be right to express their opinion. The First Amendment to our Constitution says, "Congress shall make no law respecting an establishment of religion, or prohibiting the free exercise thereof; or abridging the freedom of speech, or of the press."

That gives us the right to speak up because of our faith, and God urges us to do so. Our hope is to plant the seeds that encourage others to become faithful. Then let the Holy Spirit take over. Jesus tells us no one comes to the Father except through Him *(John 14:6)*. Those are pretty powerful words, and the "path to Heaven is narrow." But there is a stronger commandment –

You want free speech: let's see you acknowledge a man who is going to make your blood boil, who would advocate at the top of his lungs that which you would spend a lifetime opposing at the top of yours.

the greatest commandment is to love others, regardless of their viewpoint. *You have heard that it was said, 'Love your neighbor and hate your enemy.' But I tell you, love your enemies and pray for those who persecute you, that you may be children of your Father in heaven (Matthew 5:43-44).*

Others have the right to express themselves, too. Our faith becomes stronger as we defend it, because we become even more convinced of the truth. *Blessed is the one who perseveres under trial because, having stood the test, that person will receive the crown of life that the Lord has promised to those who love him (James 1:12).*

Love America. But, even more importantly, love Americans: all of them, including those who are committed to other causes.

Scripture: *Love the Lord your God with all your heart and with all your soul and with all your mind and with all your strength. The second is this: 'Love your neighbor as yourself.' There is no commandment greater than these (Mark 12:30-31).*

Question: Can you love people with opposing points of view? How can you develop harmonious relationships with people whose opinions are different than yours? Can you respectfully remain true to your faith when respectfully being in the presence of others with a differing point of view?

Prayer: Heavenly Father, teach us to love other people, even those with a different point of view. Give us the courage to enthusiastically speak of the difference faith has made in our lives, and then let the Holy Spirit do the rest. Amen.

Topic: Making a
Difference

It's a Wonderful Life

The Jimmy Stewart movie, It's a Wonderful Life, is a classic. The key character, George Bailey, has great aspirations as a high school graduate in small town Bedford Falls. Full of vitality, he wants  to leave Bedford Falls behind and pursue a new and exciting life. He wants to build tall buildings, travel the world, and go to college. As he is ready to board the train out of town his life takes a different turn. His father's family-owned bank faces a take-over crisis at the very time his father passes away. Because George has already shown that he will stand up to outside financial pressures, he is asked to step in and serve as its bank executive. George knows that if he doesn't the bank will be dissolved. As the Depression begins to set in, a greedy bank board member wants nothing more than to foreclose all its outstanding loans and take advantage of the community. When the bank is stormed during the stock market crash, it is George Bailey who personally convinces depositors not to panic and to work together. As a result they all survive the Depression. The town survives. Indeed, it thrives.

In spite of his desire to pursue his own worldly goals he stays in Bedford Falls and makes a difference in the community. Throughout his youth, there were dramatic events when George rescued his younger brother in an icy pond, and saved the life of a sick little boy when he realized that a pharmacist incorrectly filled a prescription.

Yet, George was frustrated with his unmet goals. George reached the point when he wanted to take his own life. Just before jumping off a bridge he was met by a guardian angel. George told the angel he wished that "he never had been born." The angel granted him a look at the results of his wish - a brother who drowned in the icy pond, the youngster died from the erroneous prescription, and a town left in ruins because of a greedy, heartless businessman. George Bailey's life made a major difference in Bedford Falls.

Although we may not be satisfied with some aspects of our lives, we each have made the difference in the lives of others. How different would your life have been without each family member - a son, a daughter, and a spouse? What joys would we be missing? Would your place of work be different without you? The warm smile, the feelings of acceptance you give to others all have a positive influence on others.

The role of each of us was all planned. *Psalm 139* tells us of God's intricate plan for your life. *For you created my inmost being; you knit me together in my mother's womb. I praise You because I am fearfully and wonderfully made.* And in *Jeremiah 1:5* God said, *Before I formed you in the womb I knew you, before you were born I set you apart.* That tells you God has a plan for your life. The plan might be different from our own, but as the movie It's a Wonderful Life shows us, His plan is the right one. Each one of us is precious and wonderfully made. Be satisfied with God's plan for your life. And, take pride in what His plan has done for others through you. Your life *has* been worthwhile and appreciated by others. It's a wonderful life!

Question: What difference would someone say you made in their life?

Prayer: Heavenly Father, You made each of us for a purpose. In spite of our disappointments, we have done some helpful things for others. We thank you for the opportunity to make a difference for others. Amen.

Topic: Opportunity

The Unsinkable Titanic

 The 882-foot <u>Titanic</u> luxury liner left its Southampton, England port on April 8, 1912. Embarking on her maiden voyage, her 2,200 passenger list included some of the wealthiest people of its time. Her destination was New York City. Late on the evening of April 14 the ship struck an iceberg 375 miles south of Newfoundland and sank 2 ½ hours later. Tragically, only 700 passengers survived the catastrophe.

Disasters reveal the true character of people, both good and bad. Stories survive about wealthy passengers bribing crew members for seats on lifeboats, as the ship only had enough lifeboat seating for less than half the passengers. Some lifeboats left the sinking ship with empty seats, as some people, fearing an overload would sink it, pushed off from the mother ship before reaching capacity. Only 31 percent of the crew and 32 percent of the third-class passengers survived. Clearly, social standing and duty affected the survival rate.

The overly confident crew ignored the dangers of icebergs, with its most lethal cutting force below the surface of the icy North Atlantic waters. After all, the Titanic was touted to be unsinkable. Within hours the band was playing "Nearer My God to Thee" to the remaining, doomed passengers still on board.

Are we overconfident, feeling like we can handle anything that comes our way? Do we feel like we are above the rules which really are intended for others? Do we feel superior to others? Do we overlook problems that turn out to be much greater than we ever imagined?

God doesn't care about your social status or the size of your bank account. He cares about the attitude of your heart. In due time, he will reward those who put others first. The time to sing "Nearer, My God to Thee" is before a crisis hits. We only get one maiden voyage on this earth, and you have already set sail. Prayerfully deal with the issues you see and seek God's wisdom in all areas of your life so that larger, hidden issues will not bring you down.

The words to the song, "Nearer, My God to Thee," refer to Jacob's dream of a stairway reaching to heaven *(Genesis 28)*. The ladder Jacob saw, with angels going up and down, represents that God was with him and the angels were guarding him. The ladder foreshadows Jesus, who bridges the gulf between us and the Father. Drawing nearer to God should be our goal. Jesus is the best lifesaver of all time and our bridge to God when it is time.

Scripture Basis for the Hymn "Nearer, My God to Thee":

> *When he reached a certain place, he stopped for the night because the sun had set. Taking one of the stones there, he put it under his head and lay down to sleep. He had a dream in which he saw a stairway resting on the earth, with its top reaching to heaven, and the angels of God were ascending and descending on it. There above it stood the LORD, AND HE SAID: "I AM THE LORD, THE GOD OF YOUR FATHER ABRAHAM AND THE GOD OF ISAAC. I WILL GIVE YOU*

Bruce Boyer

AND YOUR DESCENDANTS THE LAND ON WHICH YOU ARE LYING.... I *am with you and will watch over you wherever you go, and I will bring you back to this land. I will not leave you until I have done what I have promised you"* (Genesis 28:11-13, 15).

Prayer: Dear Lord, we wish to be nearer to You. Be with and watch over us as we live here on earth, and when it is time, bring us safely home with You to heaven. Amen.

Topic: Overcoming
Adversity

Let's Roll

Do you remember where you were on September 11th, 2001? Within moments of the news breaking, people were huddled around television sets at work, at home, and everywhere. Television sets showed the horrific sight of American Airlines flight 11 crashing into the North Tower at the World Trade Center at 8:45 on a Tuesday morning. What a catastrophe. My first thought was, "How could that pilot have made such an error?" It was a direct hit into the center of the tower. The second strike came at 9:03 AM. United Airlines Flight 175 crashed into the South Tower. Suddenly, there was no question that an organized assault on the United States was underway. The immediate question in all our minds became, "How many more airplanes were aimed at United States landmarks?" America was under attack.

Air traffic controllers all across the nation began to signal aircraft to land as quickly as possible. Any pilot who did not respond to communications from air traffic controllers became a suspect: was the plane being piloted by a terrorist? United Airlines Flight 93 became a prime suspect. It left Boston's Logan Airport, bound for San Francisco, but changed to a collision course with Washington, D.C. As we later found out, terrorists had killed the flight crew and aimed the aircraft at the nation's capital. The time was 10:10 AM.

Todd Beamer, a young salesman on a business trip, was aboard United Airlines Flight 93. Todd was a man of faith and a great family man with a wife, Lisa, two children at home, and one more on the way. He attended Bible study classes and was a popular adult leader of youth groups at his church. He was everything you could hope for in a loving, caring human being. God had blessed him richly.

Onboard Flight 93 Todd organized a small group of passengers to surprise the terrorists and try to retake the aircraft. Todd used the Airfone on the seatback in front of him, reaching GTE supervisor Lisa Jefferson. Todd provided information to Ms. Jefferson about the hijacking and then, together, they recited the Lord's Prayer. Todd then uttered the now famous words, "Let's Roll," put the phone down with the line still open, and sprang into action. Their actions prevented the plane from reaching the US Capitol. It crashed in an open Pennsylvania field, killing all aboard, but saving thousands of lives in the path ahead.

One of my favorite books is Lisa Beamer's account of the events of that day. Let's Roll provides insight into what happened on the doomed flight thanks to Todd's phone call. But Todd Beamer's action on that flight is only the beginning of the story. The motivational part of the story is how Lisa Beamer reacted in the aftermath of the crash. She found the confidence to go on in the face of such a tragedy and loss. It is a book of hope and inspiration, showing God to be her source of strength.

Lisa viewed the roughly 3,000 who died on 9/11 to be not just victims, but people who touched the lives of many during their time on this earth. According to her, "Their lives are of eternal value to others." The end of the story is not the memories of those who perished but one of sacrificial action. We all should do what we can for others with the time God gives us. Live like there is no tomorrow.

We all face tragedies during our lives such as facing the loss of loved ones, the loss of health, or some other event that shakes our world. No one is immune from traumatic situations. Tragedies are a test of faith, and they can be a testimony of how people draw upon God's strength to get through those situations. How does faith help you through the difficult times?

Lisa Beamer is a prime example. She exhibited inner strength, but 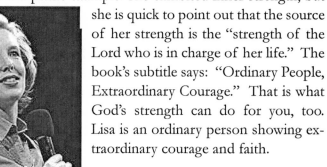 she is quick to point out that the source of her strength is the "strength of the Lord who is in charge of her life." The book's subtitle says: "Ordinary People, Extraordinary Courage." That is what God's strength can do for you, too. Lisa is an ordinary person showing extraordinary courage and faith.

Lisa commented that she has "no idea how people without faith can possibly make it through a crisis like this." It is hard enough for people with a deep faith to find peace in the face of disaster. People of faith are surrounded by positive-thinking friends who are willing to help. People of faith know where their loved one is headed. People of faith know that God will help them recover from the emptiness of such a loss. On the other hand, people who don't know the Lord don't have the same hope for the future.

She closes her book with familiar verse from *Isaiah 40:30-31*, which talks about the source of her strength:

> *Even youth grow tired and weary, and young men stumble and fall;*
> *But those who hope in the Lord will renew their strength.*
> *They will soar on wings like eagles;*
> *They will run and not grow weary; they will walk and not be faint.*

And we can learn from how she dedicates the book:

> *To Todd, my husband, my everyday hero.*
> *Thank you for loving God, loving us, and always playing hard.*
> *Thank you for teaching me patience and mercy.*
> *I love you and promise to finish our journey well.*
> *See you later …*

In the face of tragedy and loss of a loved one, know that with God's help we can finish our journey well. Death is not the end and Satan does not win. Because of our faith, we will see our loved ones later. But now, it's time for action. Let's roll!

Question: How does being a person of faith help you deal with the difficult events of your life?

Prayer: Dear Lord, we pray we will be able to have peace as we overcome difficult times in our life. With your help, Lord, we can be ordinary people with extraordinary courage. Amen.

This devotion is based on the inspirational book, <u>Let's Roll: Ordinary People, Extraordinary Courage</u>, by Lisa Beamer, Tyndale Publishing, 2002.

Topic: Passion for
a Cause

Going The Extra Mile

Kernersville used to be known for a character called "Dancing

Kenny." He is there to attract attention to local stores in that area. His dancing is enthusiastic. Rain, shine and even in brutal summer heat, the dancer performs to the music
playing on his headphones. He usually holds
a sign but sometimes he puts it aside to allow
even more expression into his dance routine.
When people honk their horns he flashes a
winning smile, waves, and adds more energy
to his dance. He obviously enjoys what he is
doing.

Recently I saw him do something very interesting. Before beginning his dancing for the day, he took time out to mow the grass in
that entire area. Most of the dancing is done at a single spot which
long ago he wore down to the bare dirt. Yet, on this day he took
the time to mow the entire area near his performance spot. The
guy wants to make a good appearance and go above and beyond
what was expected of him. He didn't have to do that – the peo-

ple watching his dancing are oblivious to the height of the grass around him. All eyes are on him because he is entertaining. To the dancer, it is much more than attracting customers. His passion takes it to an entirely different level.

So what are you passionate about? If you had one thing in life that you were really good at, do you go to extremes to make it all it can be? How did you get good at it? God gave you abilities to be really good at something, and your passion for that activity, job, or service really shows in the way you are willing to go the extra mile.

It doesn't matter what your passion is. Perhaps it is gardening, and your backyard is beautiful enough to be featured in a magazine. Maybe it is singing, and you share that gift with everyone at church. Maybe your passion is the gift of service, and you go out of your way to do things for others. It could be kindness, and you are the friend that someone really needs. Your passion doesn't have to be entertaining, but instead, serving the Lord by serving people. The list of possibilities is endless, but so are the results that come from using what God has blessed you with. God gave you unique abilities for a purpose – a purpose that makes a difference in this world. When your passion and heavenly purposes meet, you are serving the Lord.

Colossians 3:23 says, *Whatever you do, work at it with all your heart, as working for the Lord, not for men. ... It is the Lord Christ you are serving.* When your passion is spiritually motivated, you have the power of God behind you. Be passionate about what you do in the Lord's behalf, because God is passionate about you. Make it your best work – because *you* are his best work. Mow the grass and do the extra things that show your love for others, in response to God's love for you. God doesn't place limits on His love for us, so we should not limit our love for others. Go the extra mile. It's all about the heart – from God's heart to yours, and yours lovingly to others.

Touchpoints of Faith

Question: What are you passionate about? How do you use
that passion to serve others?

Prayer: Heavenly Father, we thank you for the abilities You
gave each of us. Let us enthusiastically use those
abilities to serve others. Amen.

Bruce Boyer

Topic: Inner Peace

Inner Peace

I recently read a newspaper editorial about former President Jimmy Carter. Carter has been diagnosed with a cancer that spread to  numerous parts of his body, including the brain. The article described Carter as handling his health situation with "humility and gratitude for the opportunities and privileges he has enjoyed, but the inner peace he exuded." Carter has always been considered a man of faith. Did that faith shield him from the affliction of cancer? Not at this time. Did that faith protect him from criticism that goes along with political office? No one can do that in our secular world. Carter doesn't get his strength from fellow human beings. Carter is able to handle his struggles because he is at peace with God.

A newspaper editorial highlighted the inner peace Jimmy Carter feels. Carter's service to the poor has been well documented, especially with Habitat for Humanity homes he helped build. The article also talks about worship services held at Camp David during his presidency. It was attended by members of Carter's family, staff and invited guests – many of whom didn't otherwise attend church. It talks about his involvement at his Washington church, often leading Sunday School lessons. He has had a positive influence on the spiritual lives of others.

The inner peace also refers to Jimmy Carter's contentment even in the face of an illness that may claim his earthly life. For Carter, death is not the end, but a new beginning. At the right time God will welcome the faithful into an eternity with Him.

Inner peace is God's way of taking on *our* burdens of life. We act on our faith, doing what is reasonable; and then turn it over to God. Let *God's will* be done.

Inner peace isn't reserved only for the end of life, but also for our daily struggles. Inner peace is living your life knowing "who" you are, and "whose you are." Inner peace is being grounded in faith and enjoying the synergy of believers who gather at church, supporting each other in good times and bad.

We see an entirely different world in the newspapers and on television. TV news typically reports 29 minutes on the bad things happening in the world, and then tries to end its broadcast on a positive note with a one minute feel-good story. With that ratio it is no wonder people perceive the world in a largely negative way. Satan seems to be at work nearly everywhere we turn. So how does a Christian overcome the negativism and live in peace? How do we maintain faith in a loving God when our earthly world tries to convince us our world is going to hell? Perhaps the answer to that is our goal of being in the presence of God when our time is up in this world.

Think back to Jimmy Carter. He has constantly served God by serving people. As President he saw the worst in people. The things he knew, much of which was confidential from the public, was far worse than the 6:00 pm news. Yet, he retained his faith and put it into action by helping others. As the newspaper editorial reported, Jimmy Carter was preparing himself for the new beginning. We should, too. Carter said, "If we subjugate our lives to

God, if we open our hearts to the Holy Spirit, if our life is consistent with the purpose or example of Christ ... in our relationship with God, and others, then we will have inner peace."

Giving it up to God can be difficult for people who want to be in control. God is infinitely more powerful and wiser than we are. Trust Him.

So in your quest for inner peace in the midst of chaos:

- Let faith be your guiding light, living in communion with Him, knowing you are a child of God, and are loved by the Creator.
- Ask God what he wants you to do and listen for His answer.
- Act on God's wishes, loving and forgiving others. Use the skills He gave you to serve others.
- Then put it in God's hands. Let "thy will be done."
- Surround yourself with people of faith, in public worship and in your daily life. Seek people who will support your commitment to trust God's answer.
- Allow yourself to rest and recharge.
- Trust that God's answer is the right answer; never let go of your faith as you prepare for the new beginning.

God can do wonderful things, so **let it go,** and live with peace in your heart. *And the peace of God, which passes all understanding, shall guard your hearts and minds in Christ Jesus (Philippians 4:7).* Then you can prepare for what God has in store for you, in this world and the next.

Scripture: *... And surely I am with you always, to the very end of the age (Matthew 28:20).*

Question: What steps do you take to seek inner peace, in the midst of this chaotic world?

Prayer: Dear Lord, we don't understand it at times, but

help us to live in peace in spite of the chaos all around us. Help us to center our thoughts on You and what You want us to do, and give us peace. Amen.

Acknowledgment: The quotes for this devotion are from a column written by Cal Thomas entitled "Jimmy Carter's Peace.", and published on page A15 in the <u>Winston-Salem Journal</u> on August 26, 2015.

Topic: Your Personal Savior

He Hasn't Asked Me Yet

The weekend I planned to ask Kathy to marry me I made a visit to her hometown in Missouri. It was to be more than just a Thanks-

giving celebration with her family. Kathy suspected the proposal was coming, so she guarded the door to the basement when both her dad and I were downstairs. This was "the conversation" with her dad before I would ask Kathy to marry me. I spent hours talking to him, going over the life I planned with Kathy. I told him about my anticipated career path and goals for the future. I wanted to reassure him I would be able to care for his daughter. I was very thorough, and thought I had all the bases covered. I presented Kathy with the ring later that weekend. Planning for the wedding began.

Fast forward now to the night of the wedding rehearsal. While the pastor was walking us through the ceremony, Kathy's dad was checking out the decorations in the back of the sanctuary. Then the pastor came to the part of the ceremony where the father is to give his daughter away. The pastor said, "Leon, this is when I will ask, Who giveth this woman." Without a moment's hesitation Leon said with a loud voice, "I don't know. He hasn't asked me yet." All eyes immediately shifted to me as I turned beet red.

Have you done all the right things with your life at church but failed to ask Jesus to be your Lord and Savior? Do you attend church, Sunday School and participate in many church activities, but have not actually asked God the important question? Just being present doesn't cut it. You are seeking a commitment with God, not just participation in the activities. God is waiting for you to ask the central question – to be your personal Lord and Savior. You certainly don't want to come to the moment of truth without asking God for a formal relationship.

Will God say, "I don't know. He hasn't asked me yet?"

My moment of truth came as I was standing at the altar, at the wedding rehearsal. Leon had a great sense of humor, just waiting for the right moment to show it. Even though I tried to cover all the key points well in advance, I hadn't asked the simple, key question. Leon wanted the opportunity to say "yes." And so does God.

Question: Have you asked Jesus to be your Lord and Savior?

Scripture: *If you declare with your mouth, "Jesus is Lord," and if you believe in your heart that God raised Jesus from the dead, you will be saved (Romans 10:9).*

Prayer: We ask you, Jesus, to be our Lord and Savior. You are the Son of God, whom He has raised from the dead to take away our sins, and to provide the hope for eternal life with you. We want you in our lives forever. Amen.

Bruce Boyer

Topic: Perspective

Superficial Rivalries

College and professional sports take away our objectivity and make
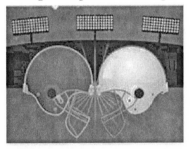 a sense of community unity more
difficult. If you live in the Caroli-
nas, wear a Duke or Carolina shirt
in public and you immediately get a
strong positive or negative reaction
from strangers you meet. People
judge you based on the logo of the
shirt you are wearing, not because
of your character. The greater the
rivalry, the stronger the opinion about the other person. Having
the upper hand can give a false feeling of power and superiority
over others. It can create animosity between people.

The morning after the opening ceremonies of the recent Winter
Olympics I read many negative Facebook posts about Russia, the
host nation. Perhaps fueled by the news media, the sentiment was
how superior the US was to our Russian competitors. The Opening Ceremony highlighted a depiction of Russian history through
a motivational video and exhibitions on the floor of the indoor
stadium in Sochi. Instead of celebrating the Russian people, we
looked for glitches in the video presentation as if that was really

important. The newspaper showed pictures of a bathroom door an American athlete punched through to get out because the door wouldn't open. According to the media, poor construction on the part of the Russian workers was to blame. Or maybe the door just locked. It doesn't matter to the media. This was a chance to show our nation as superior to another. Why do we need to do that?

Sometimes we forget that God created the Russians, Duke fans, Carolina fans, Buckeyes and Wolverines. He created Democrats and Republicans. Perhaps people think God must love you more because of the team you are on or the political party of your choosing. Nothing could be further from the truth. God loves all of His creation.

It doesn't matter how you choose to list the differences between one people vs. another, we are all creations of the one true God. That should tell you something. The only true separation God is interested in is the believers from those who do not yet believe. Instead of lifting ourselves up as superior, what God wants us to do is to love and embrace those who have not yet accepted Jesus as their Lord and Savior. Anything else is unimportant by God's eternal criteria. The rivalry for our soul is the most important of all. Satan is making his bid for people's allegiance. Working to increase the believers is where we should put our best effort. It involves loving people for whom they are, and encouraging them to be what God hopes they become. Instead of pretending to be superior, God wants you to interact in love from a servant heart position.

Don't try to judge a person's heart by the name on their shirt. Let them have fun cheering for their favorite sports teams but encourage them to have a real allegiance to God's team. One doesn't really matter, while the other matters for all eternity. We won't convince everyone to believe, but we can impress others with our loyalty to our God. The rest really isn't all that important. Let the games begin.

Question: Can I look objectively and lovingly at people with different goals than me? Does God's love for all people show through my actions?

Scripture: *That all of them may be one, Father, just as you are in me and I am in you. May they also be in us so that the world may believe that you have sent me (John 17:21).*

Prayer: Lord, You created all people. Although we may have superficial differences, help us to love everyone in Your creation. Amen.

Topic: The Power of
God's Word

The Saving Power of the Bible

It was late afternoon on a cold November 13, 1944, near the French  village of Ancerville. Foot soldiers from the 315th Regiment, Company G, were on a mission to reach the Vosges Mountains in an effort to retake Paris from the Nazis. Infantry foot soldiers were accompanied by a French tank when they were ambushed. A young American soldier named William H. "Doc" Long was part of that regiment. Long saw a bazooka shell headed for the tank. It did minimal damage to the tank, but Long was able to alert the tank to the origin of the heavy artillery fire. However, Long was hit in the right shoulder by gunfire, falling to the ground under the French tank. Only through quick action was he able to push his body free of the tank tracks as it returned fire. Lying on the ground, Long was hit again by shrapnel, this time to his left arm.

Doc Long would spend the next 18 hours lying completely still as other wounded soldiers screamed for help. Gradually those screams lessened as many of his fellow soldiers succumbed to their injuries. Once daybreak came, movement would alert the Nazis that there were still Americans alive on the battlefield.

Throughout the night Long would recite the *23rd Psalm*: *Yea though I walk through the shadow of the valley of death, I will fear no evil, for thou art with me, thou rod and staff, they comfort me. You prepare a table before me in the presence of my enemies...Surely goodness and mercy shall follow me all the days of my life, and I will dwell in the house of the Lord forever.*

Even though Doc Long was in the shadow of the valley of death, God was with him. Faith brought Doc comfort even in the presence of German troops nearby. God saw to it this wasn't to be Doc Long's last day on this earth.

There is more to the story that illustrates God's protection of Doc  Long so that we might better understand God's power. Long had in his pocket a Bible given to him by his Aunt May. When he first entered the service his aunt told him, "Please read this every day and carry it over your heart." Doc Long did read it daily and he placed it in a shirt pocket over his heart. After being rescued and taken to the first aid tent, his personal effects were returned to him. One of those personal items was his Bible. The Bible had a hole blown almost all the way through by shrapnel from enemy fire. The Bible literally saved his life.

Fortunately, most of us are not risking our lives fighting on a battlefield with our nation's freedom at stake. We are not on the front lines of World War II with enemy fire all around us. Instead, we are on the front line of the 21st century. We live in a fast-paced world that is at war in so many ways. Instead of a Bible we carry cell phones in those pockets. Instead of Nazi snipers ambushing us, the Christian faith is under attack from all sides. The unchanging values of the Bible are being challenged by a world with different values. Instead of love unifying us, we are a nation and world divided. The Bible is the force our world needs to guide us, yet it is constantly under attack. God will be with us as we stand up to the challengers of our faith. Jesus assured us by saying, *And surely I am with you always, to the very end of the age (Matthew 28:20)*.

The Bible is our protection, illuminating the path God wishes for us as well as the forgiveness we need when our human nature causes us to fall short. Even more than that, our Bible shows us the way to salvation: to the eternal life that we seek as Christians; to the life beyond the earthly battles we face. Doc Long also sought eternal life. His Bible was the guide to his human life, and also his hope for eternal life. Reading it was a natural part of his daily routine. Doc Long was willing to put his life on the line to protect freedom throughout the world. He kept his Bible over his heart because he had a heart for God. God demonstrated his love for Doc Long by using the very instrument of his faith to physically save Doc's life. God's message was clear. Believe in me and you will live.

Is reading and living by God's word important to you? Do you carry God close to your heart? If you do, God will reward your faith now and forever more. Doc Long's Bible protected him and saved his life. Our Bible is our protection and leads to us being saved.

Prayer: Heavenly Father, we thank You for people willing to sacrifice for the freedoms we enjoy. We thank You for giving us the strength to do the right thing because we know You are with us, just as You were with Doc Long. We thank You for the protection of Doc Long and other people of faith, and we know that protection is available to us if we place our complete trust in You. In Christ's name we pray. Amen.

Editor's Note: This is a true story told with permission of Doc Long and his family.

Bruce Boyer

Topic: Prayer

Laundry List

My daughter is a professional actor in New York City. Throughout

her career she has had many roles, some
as a lead, some as a supporting actor,
and some as a member of an ensemble.
In every role she had a specific job, perhaps a line to say, a song to sing, or just
a position to hold on the stage. Each
contributed to portraying the message
of the show. Each role had a purpose,
no matter how large or how small her
presence on the stage.

Every day I say prayers, not only about my own family but others,
too. Many times prayer time is lengthy – a laundry list of requests
for God's intervention. I am sure God is used to hearing such long
lists of prayers from people.

Then it hit me. Prayer is not *telling* God what you want Him to do,
but instead, asking Him for guidance on what He wants you to do
to help others in their time of need. Like the actor on the stage, I

have a real life role in the entire process. God gives me lines to say and roles to play on the stage of life. He equips me to be a friend people need when they are facing a crisis or a time of disappointment. I can step up and do something for someone who physically can't accomplish a task. A kind word can go a long ways toward a person knowing that other people do care about them, and they aren't alone in their struggles. Prayers are not a "to do" list for God, but instead are a two-way conversation on how God and I can work together to meet people's needs.

There certainly are things that only God can do. God has the wisdom to know the difference between wants and needs expressed in prayer, and He answers prayers with the big picture and perfect foresight. His answer is the right answer. If God chooses to work through us, He gives each of us the ability to do more *through Him* than we could ever hope to accomplish on our own. That is why it is important to listen for what He wants us to do.

So how do we know what God wants us to do? I am a strong believer that the Holy Spirit speaks to us at the right time. The Holy Spirit is the voice inside my head that sends me into action. I also feel another aspect of the Holy Spirit is God descending into another person. We may open the door by encouraging a person to seek a relationship with God, but then God takes over. While we may model how God has helped us, it is God who opens a person's heart to accept Him as their Lord and Savior.

You can play a role – whether big or small – in helping a person in their time of need. The next time you start to verbalize your laundry list of requests to God, stop. Listen for God to tell you what part He wants you to play. It will be an important part, and it will make a difference in someone's life. God will applaud your effort at the final curtain.

Scripture: *The heartfelt counsel of a friend is as sweet as perfume and incense (Proverbs 27:9).*

Now there are different kinds of spiritual gifts, but it is the same Holy Spirit who is the source of them all. There are different kinds of service in the church, but it is the same Lord we are serving. There are different ways God works in our lives, but it is the same God who does the work through all of us (1 Corinthians 12:4-6).

Question: What is the key part of your prayer life – talking or listening? By lengthening the time you listen do you think you and God will be more in sync?

Prayer: Dear Lord, help us to listen when we pray so that you can tell us what you want us to do. Amen.

Topic: Purpose

God's Mission for You

My all-time favorite movie is <u>The Sound of Music</u>. I love the

thought of Maria on the top of that Austrian mountain just outside Salzburg, spinning around as she sings, "The hills are alive with the sound of music." I love inspirational music and I appreciate the beauty of the Alps. I also appreciate the purity in people, which was certainly depicted by both the real Maria and the pure voice and wonderful character of Julie Andrews.

Think about the compelling storyline of the movie. Maria is seeking to be a nun, entering a convent to give her life to God. Maria is a free spirit with a special sparkle about her. God created Maria to be even more than a person willing to dedicate her life sequestered in prayer and study as a nun. God wanted to share her loving spirit with the world. Mother Abbess recognized this, and sent Maria to experience life as a governess at the home of the widowed naval officer, Captain Von Trapp. As we all know, Maria falls in love with the Captain, a man struggling between the loyalty to his homeland, the Austria he used to know, and his orders to serve the Nazi regime that had taken over Austria in World War II. The free spirited and loving Maria is afraid of her developing love for the principled Captain, and flees back to the convent. She is sent back to the Von Trapp family, and eventually marries the captain and cares for his seven children. As the Nazi's close in on Captain Von Trapp, the entire family escapes to neighboring Switzerland. Their flight is assisted by the nuns in the abbey, who admit they "sinned" by disabling the German automobile searching for the Von Trapp family.

Isn't this like our life today? Life is not simple, and has challenges coming at us from all directions. Our world is not what it once was. New demands put us in conflict with what we think is right. We want to serve God, but hiding in the safety of a convent to avoid facing them is not an option. Like Maria, we have a restlessness longing to experience life to the fullest.

If we look, we will find we can love God and serve Him in so many ways in spite of the challenges. Like Maria Von Trapp, this includes serving Him through our families; but that, too, has competing influences demanding our time and attention. There are plenty of detours, most of which are not our own doing. But keeping focused on the goal, we can find our way.

The Sound of Music is a classic more than 50 years old. Watching it, we still can feel the emotion during the twists and turns of the storyline. Lisel, "16 going on 17," loves Rolf, but he is a member of the Nazi's Third Reich. Captain Von Trapp loves his children but is too busy for them. He eventually realizes the importance of family. In his remorse over his deceased wife and the direction of his homeland, he shuts the joy of music out of his life. He is eventually inspired by his children singing the words to one of his country's most emotional songs. The flower, Edelweiss, thrives in a rocky, unforgiving soil. How symbolic is that? "Bless my homeland forever."

Now, how about you? Don't deny joy when facing severe challenges. Through God there is hope. Aren't we often too busy for our children? How do we break the cycle?

The Sound of Music is a story about courage and hope, in the face of danger, oppression, and change. It took one person, empowered by God, to be the catalyst for change. You can be that person for someone else in need. Maria changed Captain Von Trapp's relationship with his children from militaristic to loving. She changed the captain's outlook from disappointment to one of hope for a future even if it involved climbing a mountain to freedom. In the process of helping everyone else, Maria changed her own outlook from frustration and hiding to being what God made her to be, enriching the lives of everyone around her. It was all done through God's love: "A dream that will need, all the love you can give, every day of your life, for as long as you live" (Lyrics from the song "Climb Every Mountain").

You can be that catalyst for change around you and discover what God meant for you to be. *For we are God's handiwork, created in Christ Jesus to do good works, which God prepared in advance for us to do (Ephesians 2:10).*

"Climb every mountain ... follow every rainbow, 'til you find your dream."

Scripture: *He has saved us and called us to a holy life—not because of anything we have done but because of his own purpose and grace. This grace was given us in Christ Jesus before the beginning of time (2 Timothy 1:9).*

Many are the plans in a person's heart, but it is the LORD'S PURPOSE THAT PREVAILS (PROVERBS 19:21).

For I have come down from heaven not to do my will but to do the will of him who sent me (John 6:38).

Question: Have you served in a role where you have helped someone see life in a more positive way? Watching their transformation, how did if affect you?.

Prayer: Help us, dear Lord, to find ways where we can help others to improve their outlook on life. Guide us to be helpful to others and grow in our faith as well. Amen.

Topic: Pursuit of Perfection

Unlimited Ice Cream

My wife had been away for nearly two weeks, caring for her dad following eye surgery. As a result I had free rein on the selection of foods during her absence. I am a guy who likes ice cream so I hustled off to the store to purchase a half gallon of my favorite flavor. For several days I had ice cream twice a day – dessert after one meal and an evening snack. You would think I had died and gone onto heaven, as I could have my favorite food as often as I wanted. There was no one to wisely tell me "no."

It makes me wonder what life would be like if everything was perfect. There would be no one telling me what to do; no one telling me what I couldn't eat; no one looking after me who cared about my health, and steered me away from poor choices. There would be no drama or stress to cause me to worry. It would be living a life with no rules. Sound good?

Life is not like that. Every day there are challenges. We have ill-ness and injury. We make poor decisions and have to live with the consequences. At times, life can be brutal and disappointing, especially with the state of the world we see on the daily news. We may even question if there is a loving God who could allow life to unfold this way. Why doesn't God take away all of the bad stuff of this world and let us live in peace, without any worries or rules to follow?

The pursuit of perfection isn't what it is cracked up to be. By the time I neared the end of my ice cream container I didn't enjoy it as much. There was no longer anything special about it. If I wanted more it was as near as the refrigerator. Routinely having everything I wanted was boring. I wanted the interaction with Kathy, even if she monitored what I ate or gave me tasks to do.

People who have everything they want are complacent. They act as if *they* are God, or they worship the stuff they accumulate, in-stead of the God who provides for us. We want more and more. Satisfying oneself becomes the goal and life becomes "all about me." Pretty selfish stuff.

If the world this side of heaven is perfect we wouldn't need to make the conscious choice to follow Jesus. We wouldn't feel the lump in our throat when we say "I do" at the altar. The birth of a child or grandchild would be just another day. Close friends wouldn't have a special place in our heart, because what matters is what's good for me. The job promotion would be ho-hum, the next step in a career we think we are entitled to anyway. There would be no joy in the birth of Christ, because who needs God when we have everything? Every event in our life would be as ex-pected: just another bowl of endless ice cream.

Instead, life has its challenges. Because of our faith our choices are governed by the 10 Commandments and the Bible becomes our guide to daily living. We put trust in a loving God who wants to see us grow in our faith. When we rely on God for strength He carries us through the situations of life. God grants us forgiveness for shortcomings and we have a purpose in life that is far greater than just what is in it for me. His peace is not the absence of stress but having a relationship with a loving God to deal with it. *Since we have been justified through faith, we have peace with God through our Lord Jesus Christ (Romans 5:1).* We appreciate the many blessings from God, and we look forward in anticipation of the best that is to come.

Scripture: *May the God of hope fill you with all joy and peace as you trust in Him, so that you may overflow with hope by the power of the Holy Spirit (Romans 15:13).*

Question: How can you overcome the pursuit of an easy life for a life filled with hope and purpose?

Prayer: Dead Lord. We appreciate the many blessings you give us because of your love for us. May we be strengthened by the times you carry us through the issues of our life as we look forward to our future in the perfect heaven above.

Topic: Recognizing
God's Answers

Never Mind, Lord

 A little 10-year old boy climbed up on the roof of his house. He wanted to see the neighborhood from 40 feet up. He nervously climbed to the peak for a bird's eye view. At this point the boy realized the danger; if he slipped off the roof he would land on the sidewalk below. He very quickly recognized it was much more difficult going down, trying to keep his balance on the downward slope.

Almost immediately disaster struck. The boy started to lean forward and lost his balance. As he rolled and skidded downward he knew he was in trouble. He said a quick prayer: "Dear Lord, please help me. Don't let me fall off this roof."

He continued his slide down the steep roof. When he reached the edge of the roof his feet went over the side and he began a freefall towards the sidewalk below. Just at that moment his belt loop caught on a nail. The boy was suspended in air, feet dangling over the side. The boy said defiantly, "Never mind, Lord, I'm OK now."

Can you relate to this story? Do you ask God to help you out of a jam, and then when the problem seemingly solves itself, you don't give God credit for the solution? Do you call on God when all else fails, or do you involve Him from the start? Do you recognize God's hand in helping you through the tough times in your life?

The statement, "Never mind, Lord, I'm OK now," is like saying to God, "I don't need you now. I got this. I can handle things just fine without you. I'll call you if I need you."

We need to learn how to recognize God's answers to our dilemma. When you ask God for help, pay attention to what happens next. Sometimes His answer is "yes," because God approves the path you wish to take. God may also say "no," because He has something better for you. It has been said, "When one door closes, another opens." The Holy Spirit may place thoughts in your mind that clarify a decision you are facing. Sometimes God works through other people to help you when you need it the most. We can feel God's approval when we have a sense of peace and certainty about a decision.

The Lord answers every prayer. Instead of "Never mind, Lord," say "Thank You, Lord."

Scriptures:
- *This is the confidence which we have before Him, that, if we ask anything according to His will, He hears us. And if we know that He hears us in whatever we ask, we know that we have the requests which we have asked from Him (1 John 14-15).*
- *Then you will call on me and come and pray to me, and I will listen to you (Jeremiah 29:12).*
- *Ask and it will be given to you; seek and you will find; knock and the door will be opened to you (Matthew 7:7).*
- *Therefore I tell you, whatever you ask for in prayer, believe that you have received it, and it will be yours (Mark 11:24).*

Bruce Boyer

Question: When have you have asked for God's intervention and how has He answered your prayer?

Topic: Resisting
Temptation

Cyber Attack

It happens when you least expect it. Someone who doesn't even know or care about you launches an attack when you are not looking. The attack is targeted at a weakness in your operating system. Even with good intentions, you may have allowed something in that looked appealing but then becomes vicious as it turns on you. Once it makes it way in, it replicates itself, attacking healthy sectors of your system. Your system initially slows down and eventually grinds to a halt. You can no longer operate. All the good work you did, all the data being stored, is now useless.

You are probably thinking I am talking about the computer system at your desk. Most of us have experienced a computer virus and may have even had to replace the entire computer or at least had to re-format the hard drive. You may have tricked by a seemingly harmless program that turned out to launch the virus.

But I am not talking about the computer virus sent to you by an unseen hacker. I am referring to the attacks of Satan, who looks for our vulnerability and attacks our weakest point. He uses every deceptive trick available to him to make the temptation look inviting. Once it becomes a part of you, it acts as a Trojan horse, hitting you when your defenses are down and then replicating itself. You initially rationalize why everything is still okay but you start slowing down as you try to cover up the mess. You lie to throw others off. Then everything falls apart and you are done. All the good you have done spirals down the drain. So, how do you keep the attacks away? In the computer world there are several solutions that work together to keep you safe. You need the best anti-virus program there is and you need to keep updating it to handle today's new attacks. And, we need to avoid clicking on something that makes our minds wander and tests the strength of our faith. So our computer is safe; what about us?

In our daily lives we need to follow the perfect teachings of Jesus Christ. We need to live by the 10 Commandments – all of them. They are the anti-virus program of our lives. We need to keep updating our knowledge base by continuing to read the Bible daily, attending Sunday School and Bible study classes. They both motivate and inform us to be ready for Satan's attacks. And we need to resist the temptation that put us to the test. Humans are weak when going one-on-one with Satan. *Lead us not into temptation but deliver us from evil (Matthew 6:13)*. That is the best advice available.

No matter how good our computer's antivirus software is, it becomes at risk the moment we turn off that protection. An unprotected mind and soul will be at risk the moment we let down our guard. Be spiritually strong but don't put yourself to the test. Know what the Lord says is the right thing to do and keep strong in the faith.

Scripture: *Submit yourselves therefore to God. Resist the devil and he will flee from you (James 4:7).*

Question: How do you resist temptations that would taunt and trick you into letting your guard down?

Prayer: Lord, we face temptations every day. Help us to avoid tempting situations and instead, rely on Your teachings to show us what You want us to do.

Bruce Boyer

Topic: Respect

Equal in God's Eyes

 Walking by the dish room at a recent YMCA conference, a friend of mine poked her head in the door and thanked the dishwashers for an excellent breakfast. She didn't know any of them but she made a point to acknowledge the efforts of employees who work behind the scenes. How often is it that entry-level employees are treated with the respect and appreciation often reserved for executives? Not often enough.

 There are no second class people -- everyone is equal in God's eyes. *He created all the people of the world from one man, Adam (Acts 17:26).*

And it is very good. And God saw everything that he had made, and behold, it was very good. And there was evening and there was morning, the sixth day (Genesis 1:31).

Some people focus their attention on the rich and famous and ignore the less fortunate. They base their judgement of a person's worth on appearance or position. *But the LORD said to Samuel,*

127

"Do not look on his appearance or on the height of his stature, because I have rejected him. For the LORD sees not as man sees: man looks on the outward appearance, but the LORD looks on the heart" (1 Samuel 16:7).

Listen to these words from James 2: *My brothers and sisters, believers in our glorious Lord Jesus Christ must not show favoritism. Suppose a man comes into your meeting wearing a gold ring and fine clothes, and a poor man in filthy old clothes also comes in. If you show special attention to the man wearing fine clothes and say, "Here's a good seat for you," but say to the poor man, "You stand there" or "Sit on the floor by my feet," have you not discriminated among yourselves and become judges with evil thoughts? Listen, my dear brothers and sisters: Has not God chosen those who are poor in the eyes of the world to be rich in faith and to inherit the kingdom he promised those who love him?*

That they all may be one, as you, Father, are in me, and I in you, that they also may be one in us so that the world may believe that you have sent me (John 17:21).

Be kind to strangers and all people. They are creations of the same God who made you. *Don't forget to be kind to strangers, for some who have done this have entertained angels without realizing it (Hebrews 13:2).* You never know the effect your kind words will have on others.

The YMCA's traditional logo has an open Bible with John 17:21 highlighted. That verse says, *That they all may be one; as you, Father, are in me, and I in you, that they also may be one in us so that the world may believe that you have sent me (John 17:21).* Let us all be one with the Lord.

Questions: Do you treat people differently because of their position? When was the last time you made an effort to greet the custodians, the dishwashers, and others? Do you go out of your way to help all people feel valued?

Prayer: Heavenly Father, Jesus was a carpenter – not a position of wealth or stature in his community. Yet He is the most honored person to ever walk this earth, showing us how to love everyone – the children, the downtrodden, the lame, and the people rejected by others. Let us love with our heart, accepting everyone as children of God. Amen.

Topic: Returning
God's Love

Helping Others in Their Time of Need

She was a nurse to dad but... we were her patients too.

We received a thank you card from the nurse who cared for my dad in his final days. As family gathered around his hospital bed we were impressed with the care given by a nurse named Sarah. Sarah was gentle, kind and comforting to Dad, always lowering her head to his level whenever she talked with him. She had a special quality about her that showed she really cared for her patients. And Dad really appreciated her, kidding with her even though he knew the end was near.

To family members gathered at the hospital, she was thorough, informative and professional. She told us what was happening, but always in a compassionate way. She was a nurse to Dad but became a friend to us. We were her patients, too.

Sarah was a recent nursing school graduate in her first year on the job. Her bedside manner and skill level indicated otherwise. Sarah overheard family members reading something I had written to Dad. Sarah commented on how warm, loving and spiritual the note was. In response, my sister presented her with a signed copy of my devotional book, which had in it a story about Dad. We also sent a note to hospital administrators about the loving care Sarah provided.

In Sarah's thank you note to us, she expressed what a blessing it was to provide care for my dad. She said, "The day that I first cared for your father was two days after my grandpa's passing. Caring for a man as special as him reminded me of my own grandpa and healed some of my grief." She went on to say, "The day of your father's passing was truly the hardest day of my nursing career." In response to our letter to the hospital she said, "I never thought I would receive such heartfelt recognition for my care that day. It has renewed my commitment to a profession that I felt called to, in order to help others and serve God. I am forever grateful to have had the opportunity to have known such a beautiful family so devoted to God." What a wonderful note from Sarah!

You never know the power of a kind word and what it will do to help another person.

People have the opportunity to be caring and compassionate in their everyday life. Ministering to people can be done in whatever field you enter. Like Sarah, it can be a "calling" from God. Sometimes healing is not possible for the patient, but the event can still provide healing of the spirit. Sarah helped *us* through this difficult time. In our own way, we helped her as well. When you get a chance, be sure to tell someone you appreciate them — professionally and personally. You never know the hurt *they* may be feeling at the same time they are serving you. You never know the power of a kind word and what it will do to uplift another person. Perhaps one small gesture of kindness will encourage a long career helping others. We truly believe God placed Sarah in our paths, at our time of need. We are grateful we were able to return that love to her.

Scripture: *Be devoted to one another in love. Honor one another above yourselves (Romans 12:10).*
A new command I give you: Love one another. As I have l oved you, so you must love one another (John 13:34).

Question: Who has God placed in your path that you can minister to, and did it end up being a mutual bless ing for each other?

Prayer: Dear Lord, we thank you for the people you place around us, especially those who radiate your love through them. We thank you for the opportunity to affirm someone else. And we pray we will never be too busy to show our appreciation to others. Amen.

Topic: Sacrifice

Treasure

There are many movies about the excitement of searching for buried treasure. Pirates are most often depicted in this role. If they find a treasure map they are off on the hunt for riches. It is a great storyline.

In *Matthew 13* Jesus shares three interrelated parables about the Kingdom of Heaven. First is the parable about a man who found a treasure hidden in a field. The man sold everything he had and bought the entire field – and its hidden treasure.

Second is the parable about a merchant looking for fine pearls. Once the merchant found the prized pearl, he sold everything he had to buy it.

Third, Jesus described the Kingdom of Heaven as a net that was let down into the sea, catching all kinds of fish. The fish were sorted, separating the good fish from the bad.

The three people in the parables are the same person. The man, the merchant, and the fisherman are Jesus Christ. Jesus gave everything he had to buy a treasure – you. He loved you that much, He invested in you at the cost of His own life. You have great value, so much so that Jesus gave up everything – for you.

What about the net? In the end, the angels will separate the people of faith from those who reject Him. Jesus has done everything He can for you. Now, it is up to you to determine in which basket the angels will place you. Heaven is the basket for the faithful.

They haven't sorted yet. You still have the opportunity to be of faith and be placed in the heavenly basket. You are worth it! Jesus gave His life for you but the decision to accept it is up to you.

Question: What does it mean to you knowing Jesus gave His life for you?

Scripture: *The kingdom of heaven is like treasure hidden in a field. When a man found it, he hid it again, and then in his joy went and sold all he had and bought that field. Again, the kingdom of heaven is like a merchant seeking fine pearls, and upon finding one pearl of great value, he went and sold all that he had and bought it. Again, the kingdom of heaven is like a dragnet cast into the sea, and gathering fish of every kind; and when it was filled, they drew it up on the beach; and they sat down and gathered the good fish into containers, but the bad they threw away. So it will be at the end of the age; the angels will come forth and take out the wicked from among the righteous, and will throw them into the furnace of fire; in that place there will be weeping and gnashing of teeth (Matthew 13:44-50).*

Prayer: We thank You, Jesus, for trading Your life for ours. We thank You for believing in us so we can choose to live in faith with

Bruce Boyer

Topic: Salvation

Left Behind

It was a stroke of good luck, having my tonsils removed just as the 1957 World Series started. In those days all World Series games were played during the daytime, so I saw every game instead of attending 3rd grade classes that October week. As a result, I became an instant Milwaukee Braves fan as they rallied to beat the favored New York Yankees in one of the greatest series comeback efforts ever. Coming from a non-sports family, I became an instant baseball fan, wanting to be like Hank Aaron, Eddie Matthews, Warren Spahn, and the other victorious Braves. Just a few months later I went to the playground wanting to get into a neighborhood baseball game: my first game ever. They started picking teams, selecting the best athletes and working their way downward until there was no one else left – but me.

Have you ever experienced the feeling of being left behind? Everyone else is chosen while you wait for your name to be called.

You consider the possibility of never being called at all.

That Saturday morning rejection motivated me to practice the game to the point where I would soon be among the first to be chosen. I was determined to never be left behind again and I worked hard so that it would never again happen to me.

The Left Behind series of books describes what our world would be like after the Rapture when the faithful are taken up to heaven before the second coming of Christ. In the first book the luckiest people were those who disappeared from earth when the Lord did his initial selection of those He was taking with Him to heaven. The rest of the series of books tells the stories of those who were left behind because their lack of faith, facing the struggles, famines, and other calamities described in the *Book of Revelation*.

The thought of being left behind is serious business, not just a childhood game of baseball. This is the real thing! This was not about my standing compared to peers on the athletic field, but instead, my standing with God. I want to be among those that the Lord calls when the time comes, and I will work hard to be ready for that time. My objective has both a personal and team dimension. It is critical that I not only strengthen my own faith but that I share it with others. It is very important that I not let my friends and family be left behind.

Go to practice every day to improve your skills and sharpen your motivation. You can be on the winning team and be among those chosen. I want to be on God's team and I want you by my side. It's not just a game.

Scripture: *Then we who are alive, who are left, shall be caught up together with them in the clouds to meet the Lord in the air; and so we shall always be with the Lord (1 Thessalonians 4:17).*

Bruce Boyer

Question: Do you know what it feels like to not be chosen? What must you do to avoid being left behind by God?

Prayer: Lord, we pray we will be with You for eternity. We pledge to be diligent in our study of Your Word and faithful to You. Amen.

Topic: Readiness

We Don't Know the Hour

The maternity waiting room at Forsyth Hospital was buzzing with anticipation. Families huddled together awaiting the birth of a new bundle of joy. Cell phones buzzed constantly as family members checked in on the progress.

After six hours in the waiting room the now familiar ring tone next to me brought the excitement we all wanted to hear for ourselves. "We have a baby," declared the proud grandfather. Everyone gathered around to see the first photo of the new baby in his family, sent to his cell phone. A minute later the same ring tone signaled more photos. New babies bring out the best in everyone. God has presented a new opportunity to add to His Kingdom.

The long wait by all the families in the waiting room was clear evidence that none of us knew the hour when the birth would occur. For us, it would eventually mean a 12-hour day in the waiting room.

Christians are waiting for Jesus Christ's return. We know Jesus will return, but we don't know when. And when he does come it will be for a different purpose – to bring the faithful with Him to Heaven. *So Christ, having been offered once to bear the sins of many, will appear a second time, not to deal with sin but to save those who are early waiting for him (Hebrews 9:28).*

For our family we rushed to the waiting room at 11 AM, when the signs pointed to an accelerated labor. *So you also must be ready, because the Son of Man will come at an hour when you do not expect him (Matthew 24:44).* We weren't alone in the waiting room. It was now past 11 PM and most of the same families we met in the morning were still in the waiting room. Who knows when God will deliver a baby into the arms of the expectant mothers? Only God knows the hour when that will happen. The same is true of the expected second coming of Jesus Christ. *But about that day or hour no one knows, not even the angels in heaven, nor the Son, but only the Father (Mark 13:32).*

Will you be ready when Christ returns? As *Hebrews 9:28* clearly tells us, this is not the time to suddenly become a believer. Jesus taught us, by example and word, how to live. He died the death that we deserve. He told us what we must do to receive eternal life. At that coming, our opportunity to come to faith will have passed. Jesus will come to take those of faith home with Him for the eternal reward.
Be ready.

Question: What steps are you taking to be ready for when Jesus returns?

Prayer: Heavenly Father. We don't know when Jesus will return to take us home, but we pray we will be ready to join You in Heaven. Amen.

Topic: Serving Him
by Serving Others

Making Your Steps Count

On a recent birthday I received a fitness watch. This particular wrist watch counts my steps, measures my heart rate, calculates calories burned and counts how many flights of stairs I climbed. It even has the capability to evaluate my quality of sleep. The device transfers the data to my computer every time I am within 20 feet of the computer and then sends me a weekly email report with the results.

Many people are motivated by exceeding goals, not just meeting them. The standard fitness goal is 10,000 steps a day for the device I wear. I never reach 10,000 steps in a day without a planned exercise, so I need to be intentional about going above and beyond my daily routine to achieve the goal. Throughout the day my fitness watch helps me achieve a weight loss goal by comparing food intake with steps. It's all about setting and reaching goals. The watch does the measurements. I check it probably 25 times a day to see how I am doing because I want to reach my goal.

How serious are you on making your life count? There is no computer program or high tech wrist watch designed to measure service to the Lord. If you rely on external incentives, there isn't anything scientific to help you serve others. In the end, God alone is the judge of our worth. He certainly doesn't want us making lists of accomplishments. He just wants us to do it because it is the right thing to do. God sees the big picture and how all the little things contribute to our overall purpose in life. The little things – kindness and helping others all add up, even though they may seem insignificant at the time. It's not just the big projects that count. Every little thing you do to help others is significant. God sees the big picture by looking at the heart. It doesn't take a specialized wrist watch to measure our "heart rate." God knows your heart and your motivation to help others.

Just as each step adds towards our wellness goal, set a goal to do all you can to serve Him by serving others. Similar to a 10,000-step goal, you won't reach it unless you make a concerted effort. Want to win and accomplish your goal? Be a servant in your everyday life. *Sitting down, Jesus called the Twelve and said, "Anyone who wants to be first must be the very last, and the servant of all" (Mark 9:35).*

Achieving one goal on the fitness watch provides motivation to do more. Seeing the appreciation of others for what you do is encouragement to do more. Because of the steps you take, others feel valued and better about themselves. The results speak for themselves – the smiles and sense of peace from the people you help. Serving Him is the only thing that counts, one intentional step at a time.

Question: How can you seek to serve others in small, seemingly insignificant ways? What major efforts to serve are you making?

Scripture: *For even the Son of Man did not come to be served, but to serve, and to give his life as a ransom for many (Mark 10:45).*

Prayer: Heavenly Father, you came to serve, not to be served. Let us do the same in the name of Jesus Christ, our Lord and Savior. Amen.

Bruce Boyer

Topic: Serving
Others' Needs

Oblivious to the World

When I exercise at the YMCA I often wear headphones, listening to music as I walk the treadmill. Being preoccupied with listening to favorite music or engrossed in an e-book takes away my awareness of the physical exercise, and makes the time go by faster. Wearing the headphones on a neighborhood walk, however, is entirely different. I may be so involved in the music I don't pay attention to traffic, especially if I am getting ready to cross the street. On a recent walk I was enjoying movie theme songs when a guy passed me going the other direction. Not only did he wave but he said something, but my music prevented me from hearing him. The music was a distraction from interaction with a neighbor.

Sometimes we go through life in a trance, unaware of the needs of others we have just walked past. We get so preoccupied that we have blinders on when it comes to other people. Open your eyes and ears to be responsive to needs or just to be a friend to someone. *If anyone has material possessions and sees a brother or sister in need but has no pity on them, how can the love of God be in that person? Dear children, let us not love with words or speech but with actions and in truth (1 John 3:18).*

God has given you the gift of health, so you can walk, run, or do whatever exercise helps you take care of the body He gave you. Enjoy the entertainment of music or e-books but keep alert to ways you can serve others. Even though they may come up at inopportune times, the needs of others are not the distraction. Don't let the preoccupation with your task be a distraction from doing God's work – taking care of His people. Your kindness shows God's love to someone else. *And if you spend yourselves in behalf of the hungry and satisfy the needs of the oppressed, then your light will rise in the darkness, and your night will become like the noonday (Isaiah 58:10).*

I recently made a comment at a meeting about the YMCA director in my home town. My comment was she spent so much time in the lobby you would think she worked the Member Services Desk. What she was doing was interacting with the members. The work on her desk could get done at another time. The people of the YMCA are her #1 priority. She serves her members first. You can still get your tasks done and give others your caring attention. Serve God first by serving others.

Faith isn't about just us spending time with God in our own little private world. Faith is having a relationship with God and then serving Him by serving others.

Scripture: *What good is it, my brothers and sisters, if someone claims to have faith but has no deeds? Can such faith save them? Suppose a brother or a sister is without clothes and daily food. If one of you says to them, "Go in peace; keep warm and well fed," but does nothing about their physical needs, what good is it? In the same way, faith by itself, if it is not accompanied by action, is dead (James 2:14-17)*

Question: Do you find yourself engrossed in your own little world and not taking the time to help others? How can you be more attentive to the needs of others?

Prayer: Dear Lord, we pray we will listen to others and respond to their needs, as You have responded to ours. Amen.

Topic: Sharing
the Faith

The Cross in My Pocket

 As I leave the house each day, one of the items that goes into my pocket is a small metal cross. It goes into my right hand pants pocket along with any loose change I might need that day. Then, when I go to make a purchase I reach into that same pocket and pull out the available change and, along with it, the cross. The main purpose of having the cross in my pocket is to casually remind *me* throughout the day whom I serve.

There are times during the day when I just reach into the pocket to assure myself it is there. The cross serves as a constant reassurance of what Jesus has done for me. Jesus Christ is with me throughout my day.

As a person who likes punny word play, I might also say that because of the cross, I am a "changed" person. What could be more symbolic than to reach into my pocket seeking to make change, and finding the cross that has changed me and so many people?

I don't know what it is about store clerks, but when I start to count the pocket change they seem to focus on what is in my hand. There have been times when store clerks have observed the cross embedded in the change. Often times, it provides an opportunity for the clerk to share their faith in the safety of being with someone else of faith.

One time recently, a clerk even said that she wished she had a cross to remind her of her faith. It became an impromptu gift to the clerk as I completed my purchase.

Whether you wear a cross on your lapel or as a necklace, or carry one in your pocket, it may create opportunities for you to share your faith with others, or for them to discuss their faith with you. What could be better than sharing the reminder of what Jesus did for me with someone else?

The little metal cross is such a small object but serves as a big reminder for us to live a life that has been changed because of the cross.

Scripture: *What this means is that those who become Christians become new persons. They are not the same anymore, for the old life is gone. A new life has begun! (2 Corinthians 5:17).*

Question: What symbols do you carry or display that tells others you are a person of faith, and are willing to discuss your faith with others?

Prayer: Dear Lord, we pray that we will have opportunities to share our faith with others. Please give us the right words to say when we have those opportunities. Amen.

Real Life Testimonial from a Friend:

After sending this devotion out I received this comment in return:

"Bruce, I seem to remember a very dark time in my life when a true friend handed me a cross just like that! It remains in my RIGHT pocket every day, to this day...and it will have been five years on October 28.

I visit a physical therapy center three times per week now. They keep a simple Styrofoam cup on their receptionist's counter, filled with exactly those crosses. I take one at each visit, with designs on sharing my "extra" one with someone before I return to pick up another.

You have made a real difference in my life, and I thank you sincerely for that!!!"

Bruce Boyer

A Community of Flowers

 A number of years ago a local businessman in our community passed away. Paul Ciener's gracious bequest was to create a botanical garden to share his love for flowers with the community. After 12 years in the making the botanical garden became a reality.

How a flower comes to be is a mystery to me. It involves preparing the soil, removing weeds and loosening the dirt. A seed is carefully placed into the earth, mixed with rich potting soil, and water is generously added. Then God takes over.

Growing faith is also a nurturing process. A person's heart must be receptive as faith won't take root in a hardened heart. We plant the seed through encouragement or example. Sometimes people are ready to consider a relationship with God at a low time in their lives. They need both the friendship of others and to feel God's love at a critical time in their lives. Other times it comes at the

149

beginning of a new chapter such as the birth of their first child or a change in relationships. The opportunity also may be during a miraculous event where people see God at work. Sometimes a person wants the peace they see in people of faith in their life.

The environment in which we live is the "soil" of the analogy. High school students are more likely to be strong in their faith if their friends are believers. That is why youth groups and wholesome activities are so important. Peers are a powerful influence that makes it okay to seek faith. Once the seed starts to grow, it won't grow to its fullest unless it is fed with a combination of meaningful worship, study, and encouragement.

A faith conceived because of a temporary need in a person's life may not last. Once the crisis is over, people may feel like they can handle things from that point on, and they don't need God. Consistent nourishment is important to build a firm foundation of faith. We have to know *what* we are having faith in. Faith is not just emotion. It is substance. It is seeking a relationship with God in both good and tough times.

We can have all these elements present but it is God who makes the seed grow. *So neither he who plants nor he who waters is anything, but only God who gives the growth (1 Corinthians 3:8).* God breathes the breath of life into the seed. Through the Holy Spirit, God knits together all these elements. We set the stage, but we don't have to do it all. God works with the opportunity we create when we plant the seed.

At the botanical garden ribbon cutting ceremony the speaker talked about the definition of a botanical garden. Part of the definition was that a botanical garden has an educational purpose. Botanical gardens help people grow in their understanding and appreciation of flowers. Strengthening our faith is also about increasing our knowledge of a God who wants us to grow into beautiful people who flourish – blossom – because of a mutual love with Jesus Christ.

A botanical garden is not one flower, but a community of flowers, each with its uniqueness and beauty. Just as the collection of wonderful colors and shapes enhance the beauty of the garden, our community of faith is enhanced by being part of something much bigger than ourselves.

Scripture: *But the seed on good soil stands for those with a noble and good heart, who hear the word, retain it, and by persevering produce a crop (Luke 8:15).*

Question: What are some of the ways you can invite others to come to faith?

Prayer: Heavenly Father, You provide beauty for us every day – in the flowers of the field and in the people all around us. Help us to plant the seeds of faith in those around us. Amen.

Topic: Sharing
Your Faith

Saving Lives

Nicolas Winton & Vera Gissing (seated) c
by Winton.

I recently saw a Facebook video that showed a man named Nicolas Winton who organized a rescue operation that saved the lives of 669 Jewish Czechoslovakian children from Nazi death camps. Winton brought them to safety in Great Britain in 1938 and 1939.

Nicholas' wife found a scrapbook with the names of the children he saved. She orchestrated an event for Nicolas to be sitting in a crowded theatre. Other than the speaker at the podium, every member of the audience was a person saved by Winton, 75 years earlier.

At the beginning of his presentation, the speaker pointed out a lady named Vera Gissing. Vera was seated in the front row, next to

Nicolas Winston. Until that moment Winton had no idea who she was, and he had saved her life at the death camp. As the speaker introduced her to Winton there were tears and hugs between the two. They both stood up to enthusiastic applause. It was then she told him that he was the only reason why she was alive today.

But there is more; much more. The speaker then asked if there was anyone else in the audience who also owed their life to Winton. When he looked around, nearly everyone in the audience stood up. Only then did Nicholas Winton realize the enormity of what he had done.

This true story brings a tear to my eye thinking one person had saved the lives of hundreds of innocent children. So how would you feel if you were surrounded by people you saved? Maybe that day will come. Picture yourself in heaven, surrounded by people you encouraged in the faith. They are there only because of you. It can happen.

Thankfully, we don't live during a world war, but there is a war of persecution going on around us. It is becoming more difficult for a person to accept Jesus Christ as their Savior. Christianity is under attack. Everywhere we turn people try to take away public mention of God. Much like Hitler, the world wants to dictate to and control us. It may be okay to talk about God behind closed doors, but public prayer, religious symbols, and any public mention of God draws objections. Without us fighting back, people will have less chance to come to know Jesus Christ as their Savior. Don't let there be an empty theatre because we didn't share God's love with others. Wouldn't it be great if God said, "Is there anyone else here who owes their eternal life to _____ (insert your name here)," and many people stood up.

Question: Do you have the courage to step out of your comfort zone and encourage others in their faith? Feel uncomfortable doing this? Not sure what to say? Let the Holy Spirit take over.

Scripture: *We are therefore Christ's ambassadors, as though God were* *making his appeal through us. We implore you on Christ's behalf: Be reconciled to God (2 Corinthians 5:20).*

But you will receive power when the Holy Spirit comes on you; and you will be my witnesses in Jerusalem, and in all Judea and Samaria, and to the ends of the earth" (Acts 1:8).

Prayer: Dear Lord, we pray our life can make a difference in the lives of others. Give us the courage to share our faith so that others may know of God's love for them. Amen.

Bruce Boyer

Topic: Gifts

Captain's Choice

Captain's Choice is a familiar format for team golf tournaments. All the players on a team hit from the same spot and the "captain" chooses which shot will be used as the starting point for the next shot. Then each player retrieves their ball and hits from the chosen spot.

As you can imagine, in a Captain's Choice golf tournament you don't have to be a good player to score well. You just have to be on a strong team with players that make up for your weaknesses. Even the weakest player in a tournament can end up on the championship team if the other players are strong.

On the course of life we have the opportunity to play on the winning team. We don't have to be a strong player, just a faithful member on God's team. God is the team captain. He distributes the gifts (abilities) and determines what contributions from each person are used to help the cause. We all have a role to play that, when combined with others, can accomplish great things. You contribute what you can but you never have to "earn" the end result. The result is given to you if you contribute as a member of God's team.

In my most recent golf tournament I was on a strong team. During the course of play I shanked some shots and clearly showed my lack of abilities in golf. There were shots that ended up in the woods but there were also some good ones right down the middle of the fairway. On one particular hole with a water hazard, my tee shot cleared the lake and was the shot of choice for our team. Amazingly, on the two toughest holes of the course it was my tee shot that put us in the best position both times. Just when you think you have nothing to give, when you try, your contribution may be just what is needed to help the team succeed. After all, God can bring out the best from you. He knows what you are capable of doing, which is far more than you think you have to give. In everyday life there are always people who can do a particular task better than you. Expecting to be the best at something is a formula for defeat. For me, trying to win at golf based on my own abilities is not realistic. But I can contribute my best effort and rely on others for strength. I can't earn a victory by myself on the golf course, or in course of life. Being on God's team, however, provides an opportunity to rely on Him for strength, with the victory assured in the end. The reward is the eternal life we all seek.

Scripture: *Whatever you do, work at it with all your heart, as working for the Lord, not men, since you know that you will receive an inheritance from the Lord as a reward (Colossians 3:24).*

Question: What contributions have you made to a team effort that helped the overall cause?

Prayer: Dear Lord, we pray we will make an effort to contribute our best effort to serving You by helping others. Amen.

Bruce Boyer

Topic: Temptation

Smoke & Mirrors

When I walked into the Sunday school class I didn't expect to see a magic show. Our instructor had lined up a series of soft drinks and asked a class member to select a drink. With everyone watching, the instructor put the chosen Coca-Cola in a paper bag, talked for a minute, and then turned the bag upside down. Instead of the bottled soft drink falling to the floor, nothing happened -- the bag was empty. The instructor wadded up the empty bag and tossed it into the waste basket. We all saw him put the Coca Cola in the bag. Didn't we?

We've all been there. We see the magician appear to be doing something, only to find out that we were deceived. What we thought was happening really didn't happen at all. We've all seen magicians pulling coins from behind someone's ear, watched swords thrust through a wooden box with a person inside. When the box was turned around, it was empty except for the sword. How did they do that? The answer is that it is all an illusion – smoke and mirrors. Our minds convince us that something has happened, while in reality we are distracted as the magician does his magic. We make an assumption based on what we were told was going to happen.

Satan works the same way. He promises you something that you really want to happen, but in reality, his promises are just illusions. Satan told us what we wanted to hear and we eagerly took the bait. We often don't check the validity of what we are told because we want what he is offering.

Remember when Satan tempted Jesus after 40 days in the desert? Satan knew Jesus was hungry, and he tried to bait Jesus. Then he promised Jesus the world. *Next the Devil took him to the peak of a very high mountain and showed him the nations of the world and all their glory. "I will give it all to you," he said, "if you will only kneel down and worship me" (Matthew 4:8-9).* With what authority can the devil promise "all this" to the son of the creator?

Like watching a magic act, are we fooled into believing something because we want something to happen? Perhaps we are looking for an easy solution to a problem. Maybe we are craving something that really looks desirable. We are tempted all the time to do something contrary to our beliefs, testing our resolve. Satan tries to justify the wrongdoing as he baits us to accept his offer. He knows all the right buttons to push as he seeks our weak spots. He can be very convincing.

Why does Satan do this? Satan wants us to question our faith. He doesn't want us to do the right thing. He wants to drag us down to his level because he doesn't want us to reach the final heavenly destination.

Stand true to your faith. Stand up against the illusion of empty promises and instead, stand up for Jesus. Be on the alert for times when you try to justify your actions just to convince yourself it is

OK. Don't give in. How do you know if something is right or wrong? The Bible provides the measure we need. When facing temptation, pray, seek the support of others and remember the purpose God has given to us. *But remember that the temptations that come into your life are no different from what others experience. And God is faithful. He will keep the temptation from becoming so strong that you can't stand up against it. When you are tempted, he will show you a way out so that you will not give in to it (1 Corinthians 10:13).*

Scripture: *Keep alert and pray. Otherwise temptation will overpower you. For though the spirit is willing enough, the body is weak (Mark 14:38).*

Question: How do you withstand temptations?

Prayer: Heavenly Father, give us the power to discern Satan's lies from Your truth, and then to withstand temptations. Amen.

Topic: Trust

Stretching to Reach a Far Greater Potential

In recent years I have suffered several athletic injuries that needed physical therapy to return to health. An evaluation by the physical therapist assessed the injury and prescribed a treatment plan. For me, that involved gently stretching the affected area to restore my range of motion. My own objective was to be able to resume my usual activities. The physical therapist had higher goals. According to a definition, physical therapy uses "exercises and equipment to help patients regain or improve physical abilities."

The big problem with stretching is my own reluctance. I had predetermined what I could do, and because of soreness from the injury, over time I even lessened my expectations. On the training table I would instinctively resist efforts to stretch beyond my self-imposed comfort zone. It is a matter of control, comfort zone, and confidence. But when I relaxed and let the therapists do their job I was able to stretch myself to higher levels, and true healing took place. My body instantly had a new, expanded range of motion. In essence, I felt like a new man.

Did you catch the part in the definition of physical therapy relating to improving physical abilities? It said, the therapist takes you *beyond* what you think you can do. We often hold ourselves back from our true potential, on the training table and in real life. If we restrict the trainer we fail to fully heal and never reach our full capacity. In our personal lives, if we trust God, He will help us reach new levels. God created us to do much more than we imagine possible.

Don't think you can do it all on your own. Injuries may never fully heal without outside intervention. You also can't reach your God-given potential by shutting God out. Allow God to stretch you to new heights, because He gifts you with so much more potential than you realize. My favorite Bible verse is *Philippians 4:13: I can do all things through Christ who gives me strength.* "All things" includes every task God asks you to do. Open your hearts to serve God. He will greatly exceed what you thought possible.

The physical therapist has both restored and increased my physical capabilities. Let God be your trainer in life: *But Jesus looked at them and said to them, "With men this is impossible, but with God all things are possible" (Matthew 19:26).*

Question: In what ways have you held yourself back, but with God's help could accomplish so much more?

Prayer: Heavenly Father, You created us to do good things in Your name. You gifted us with abilities to accomplish everything You ask of us. Let us put our faith in You and stop worrying about our own self-imposed limitations, because through You all things are possible. Amen.

Topic: Using
God's Gifts

The Perfect Gift

My parents had a corner in their attic piled with unused gifts. Some of the gifts date back to their wedding, nearly 75 years ago. For one reason or another they chose to save some of the gifts, still in their original boxes. Once my Dad purchased Mom a new car that she felt was too nice to take out on the road. We affectionately called it the "museum piece." When she passed away, the car had less than 20,000 miles and was more than 25 years old. Gasoline evaporated over time from lack of use. In essence, having the car was a waste.

Our family is very practical in gift giving. Gifts were never inappropriate or too trendy. My parents just didn't choose to use them.

Like our own gift giving, God carefully selects the gifts He wants you to have. Since He created you for a specific purpose, God knew exactly what gifts you and I need to carry out that purpose.

Do you remember what it is like on Christmas morning or at a birthday celebration, especially if you selected "the perfect gift" for someone? Waiting in anticipation for the opening of that carefully chosen gift? There is a hush in the room as everyone waits for the box to be opened. We feel as good about giving the gift as we hope the receiver is to open it.

What is it like for God? God gives us gifts with eager anticipation of what we are going to do with them. The gifts are skills, aptitudes, abilities, and people God knew would make a real difference in the world.

God is a much more thoughtful shopper than us. God has the ability to know what the future has in store for us, what opportunities we will have in our lives. God knows the situations we will encounter that will provide the perfect setting to use His gifts. God intends for us to enrich His kingdom and serve others.

Be open to opportunities that come your way. Opportunities come when we use God-given gifts to carry out His divine purpose for our lives. God places you directly in the heart of situations, equips you with abilities, and then stands with you as you carry out His plan.

God is the eager giver, gleefully waiting to see what you do with what He gives you. Please don't put them back in a box and bury them in the attic, and go on living as if God didn't exist. Your return gift to God is the joy He receives when you use the gifts to accomplish His purposes.

There will come a time when God will ask you, face to face, what you did with the gifts He has given you. Make Him happy.

Scripture: *Each of you should use whatever gift you have received to serve others, as faithful stewards of God's grace in its vari-*

ous forms (1 Peter 4:10).

Question: What gifts has God given you? How are you using those gifts to help others?

Prayer: Lord, we thank You for the many gifts You have given us. We pray we will use them in Christian service to others. Amen.

Bruce Boyer

Topic: Listening and
Learning from
the Message

The Take-Away

We went from church straight to a restaurant for our Sunday lunch. A number of people were waiting in line for a seat at the popular restaurant. As we waited to get a seat some people noticed we were dressed appropriately for church. A young lady asked if we had just been to church today. I quickly answered "yes." Of course I had been; that was obvious, I thought. Then came the question: "What did you learn in church today?" It was a simple question, but it caught me off guard. It was intended as a friendly gesture but it hit me square between the eyes. I wasn't ready to answer. Rushing from church to the restaurant I hadn't stopped to reach conclusions about what I had experienced that morning. To be honest, I stammered a bit as I tried to give an answer.

It is easy to give the pat answer to questions about church. I can communicate my faith in general terms. But, what if I am asked the direct question: What did I learn **today**? What part of the service – today – had an impact on my life? Was I engaged in the service today, or had I mentally checked out? Did I listen closely to the sermon, readings, and music so that today's service had made a lasting impression on me? And what about Sunday School? Did I learn something new there? It doesn't matter if I heard the same scripture verse for 50 or 60 years, I can understand something more fully each time it is read.

Don't attend church on auto pilot, thinking physical attendance is enough. Were you there mentally? Don't let the service be a blur in your memory bank as you begin your week.

As you exit the church next Sunday ask yourself the simple question: what did I learn in church today?" If you can honestly answer that question you will know what God is saying to you - today.

Then, go and enjoy a wonderful Sunday lunch, and perhaps awaken someone else with the question, "What did you learn in church today?"

Scripture: *Let the wise listen and add to their learning, and let the discerning get guidance (Proverbs 1:5).*

Questions: Are you actively learning in church
each week?
What did you learn in church Sunday?

Prayer: Lord, it is easy to go on auto-pilot and not truly listen to the message at church. Help us to be attentive so that we will hear what You are saying to us through worship.

Faith Lessons with a Seasonal Topic

Topic: Easter Preparation
Season: Beginning of Lent

Final Quarter

 We've probably all been there. A favorite team is involved in a furious fourth quarter rally. Sometimes we are on the winning end, and sometimes it is the other team that overcomes a big deficit to win the game. So, what decides whether or not your team wins?

The difference maker is often the level of dedication, preparation and sacrifice that went into the game. The well-coached team that has worked hard in practice has the upper hand at the deciding moment of the game.

Ash Wednesday is the beginning of the Lenten season. The 46 days between Ash Wednesday and Easter simulate the 40 days Jesus was in the wilderness. During that time the devil tempted him but Jesus never gave in. We all know that Easter is coming, with the emotional highs and lows of Holy Week ahead. Lent is like the fourth quarter in a sports contest, with the clock ticking down.

Lent is one of those unusual times of the year. We are encouraged to give up something for lent – to show our commitment and sacrifice. For many we give up certain foods that we enjoy, perhaps things we know we shouldn't have in the first place. We are also encouraged to show our commitment in other ways, such as being more diligent in reading our Bible or performing some new act of service. Remember – Jesus was in the wilderness for 40 days and never weakened.

 We know that Easter Sunday is coming. The date is written on our calendars. Even if we do nothing, Easter Sunday will eventually come and His Victory over death will be announced. We know that the church will celebrate his resurrection – with or without our commitment. It is important to know there is no Victory for us if Easter is a day on the calendar, but not written in our hearts. That's why Lent is so important. We need to prepare our hearts for His Victory, so it can be *our* victory.

We can watch a game on television and not be emotionally involved. If we don't really care who wins, it doesn't matter. Yet, if we are actively involved with the Lenten season -- preparation, sacrifice, and commitment, Easter will have much more meaning for you. Honoring Jesus' sacrifice will help us to be stronger against temptations.

Easter Sunday will come, whether or not we do anything different during Lent. The calendar pages turn at the same pace. Being indifferent to Easter will reap indifferent results. Now is the time for preparation. Increase your commitment to attend church, participate in Bible study classes and personal reading and prayer. Give up something so that you can identify with Jesus' sacrifice. That will help you realize the ultimate sacrifice Jesus has made for you. When the final horn sounds – and it will – will you have been actively involved in preparation, commitment and sacrifice so that you are in the game? Don't let the Easter resurrection be for others, and the announcement of the resurrection not be for you.

Scripture: *Yet even now, says the Lord, Return to me with all your heart, with fasting, with weeping, and with mourning; Rend your hearts and not your clothing. Return to the Lord, your God, for he is gracious and merciful, slow to anger, and abounding in steadfast love, and relents from punishing. Who knows whether he will not turn and relent, and leave a blessing behind him, a grain-offering and a drink-offering for the Lord, your God? (Joel 2:12-14).*

Question: What do you do during Lent to prepare for the resurrection of our Lord and Savior, Jesus Christ?

Prayer: Dear Lord, during this Lenten season, help us to understand the meaning behind Jesus' sacrifice and victory over death.

Bruce Boyer

Topic: Encouraging
Others
Holiday: Memorial
Day

Never Leave a Fallen
Comrade Behind

On Memorial Day we remember those who have died in our nation's service. Officially proclaimed by President Lyndon Johnson in May, 1966 (Waterloo, NY), various celebrations go back as far as 1868 when General John Logan placed flowers on the Arlington National Cemetery graves of both Union and Confederate soldiers. It is important that we remember with appreciation the supreme sacrifices people have made for our freedoms.

I recently came across the quote from the U.S. Army Ranger creed that said (paraphrased), *"I will never leave a fallen comrade."* What a noble, sacrificial gesture. When a soldier is wounded or even dead, their goal is to not let the soldier fall into enemy hands. We need to look out for each other even if it means a sacrifice on our part.

Isn't this what Jesus Christ has done for us? No matter what the circumstance, He is not giving up on fallen people. Lots of people fall to sin or unbelief and are at risk of falling into the hands of the devil. But Christ never turns his back on people when things are going badly. He is willing to restore them to good graces at the 11th hour. There are lots of times when sinful people come to faith after an extended period of time on the other side. Only God knows if their conversion is sincere and for the right reasons. Their motivation and depth of faith is not for us to judge. God wins – Satan loses – when people come to faith.

While we remember soldiers who gave their lives on Memorial Day, perhaps fighting in wars they didn't start; perhaps reflect on how the battlefield of everyday life is also a war. Satan is fully engaged in a war to win our souls. Satan fights dirty, trying to find our weak spot and attacking there. Satan is willing to do whatever it takes to pull us away from God. People who have fallen away from faith need others to encourage them to come back. That is especially true when someone is defenseless and may have given up because of their circumstances.

In our own personal and business lives, we meet many fallen comrades: people in need of a savior. Do your best to introduce and encourage each to become a person of faith. Be the beacon as you see others needing a friend. Don't give up on them, leaving them on the battlefield, exposed to the enemy. Without your help they might not make it.

The Armed Forces award medals for bravery, but the motivation for patriotic action is really just to save a fallen comrade. Helping to save a fallen comrade in the battle for their soul earns you something much more valuable than a medal. It creates the possibility of an eternal life together because you are bringing a person along with you who might not otherwise make it.

Scripture: *Do not let any unwholesome talk come out of your mouths, but only what is helpful for building others up according to their needs, that it may benefit those who listen (Ephesians 4:29).*

Question: What can you do in your everyday life to not leave people without a faith behind?

Prayer: Heavenly Father. We thank You for never giving up on us. Even though we continue to sin and have fallen short, You continue to forgive us. And, we pray we will never give up on encouraging other people to become of faith. Life is a battle with many casualties. Help us to always be there for others when they need us the most. Amen.

Topic: Forgiveness
Season: Independence
Day

Celebrating Our Freedom

This week we celebrate our country's independence with parades, fireworks and family cookouts. Our independence was an effort to seek freedom from the rule by Great Britain in the late 1700s. Thomas Jefferson and others drafted the Declaration of Independence, ratified by the Second Continental Congress on July 4, 1776. Since that time brave American soldiers have fought to protect the freedom not only of our citizens but of others around the world. The cause of freedom is worth fighting for.

We have what so many people want – freedom.

Jesus came to live on earth to show us a new way of life – that of freedom. He freed us from trying to live up to the rigid, impossible laws of Old Testament times. He taught us that we don't have to be perfect – just forgiven. *Then you will know the truth, and the truth will set you free (John 8:32).* Jesus tells us that God's truth leads to salvation and our freedom is relief from the guilt of sin. Jesus Christ suffered the consequences of our sin so we could live in freedom. Thankfully, we live in a homeland that allows us the freedom to worship a loving God, who accepts us for who we are, and helps us to move towards being what He made us to be.

One pastor who served our church closed each worship service with the words, "You are free." No matter where in the world you live, God loves you and offers forgiveness to those who ask. We all fall short, so we all need His grace. We celebrate that freedom every time we drink from the cup and eat the bread sanctified by God.

Freedom is something worth fighting for, and yet it is available anywhere in the world, merely because of our faith.

Americans celebrate Independence Day once a year. God's grace and freedom are available to us every day. Let your faith be the Ellis Island to welcome you to the freedom provided by the cross. Ask Jesus to set you free. Let the celebration begin.

Scripture: *So if the Son sets you free, you will be free indeed (John 8:36).*

Question: What difference does the freedom Jesus won for you make in your life?

Prayer: Dear Lord, we thank You for allowing us to live in freedom, both as a citizen of this country and as a believer in Your son, Jesus Christ. Amen.

Topic: Freedom through
Christ
Special Day: Memorial Day

Let Us Not Forget

 Our regard for veterans is paramount today because it is important to not forget the commitment of people who have and continue to serve in our military. We especially remember those who sacrificed their lives for our freedom. Just take a look at Arlington National Cemetery and you get a sense of the enormity of that sacrifice. Human life is the most any of us have to give.

For deceased veterans, theirs was a fight between the good and bad guys. Many fought to protect our homeland, but some fought to protect someone else's land, all in the name of freedom. Our goal is a world at peace. Ronald Reagan said with much pride in the American spirit, "Peace is the highest aspiration of the American people. We will negotiate for it; sacrifice for it; we will not surrender for it; now or forever. We are Americans."

Bruce Boyer

On Memorial Day flags are everywhere, lining sidewalks, on buildings, and even ornamenting our local YMCA. Flags give us a patriotic feeling and show our support for our military, whom have earned our respect. Flags portray an even more powerful image when you see them placed on graves, each in tribute to a person who gave their life to protect ours. *Greater love has no one than this: to lay down one's life for one's friends (John 15:13)*. On this day, let us pause in appreciation for what each American soldier has done for us. Because of them, we are free.

 Jesus Christ was God's supreme sacrifice, giving his life for our freedom. He died a cruel, inhuman death at the hands of Roman soldiers. Because of his death we may receive forgiveness and be free from the eternal consequences of sin. *It is for freedom that Christ has set us free. Stand firm, then, and do not let yourselves be burdened again by a yoke of slavery (Galatians 5:1)*. Jesus showed us the difference between right and wrong. *Then you will know the truth, and the truth will set you free (John 8:32)*. We no longer are slaves to sin. Jesus offers forgiveness of sins when we fall short. For Jesus, the peace we desire came in the form of love.

On this Memorial Day let us remember the sacrifice of so many who gave their lives for us, including those who went into battle to protect our country and the cause of freedom. Let us also always remember the sacrifice of the One who went into battle to protect our souls. Because of His love for all people, His sacrifice is for everyone, everywhere.

Question: How are our American soldiers' sacrifices for the cause of freedom similar to Jesus' sacrificial death for our souls? How are they different?

Scripture: *In him and through faith in him we may approach God with freedom and confidence (Ephesians 3:12)*.

Prayer: We thank You for people so passionate about our country they are willing to risk their lives for us, so that we will be free to live and worship You. In Christ's name we pray. Amen.

Bruce Boyer

Topic: Gifts
Special Day: Father's Day

A Precious Father's Day Gift

A recent Father's Day was particularly special for me. Not only do I get to talk with my grown children but the third literally put on a show for me. At the time my daughter was performing as Patsy Cline at a theatre in Pennsylvania. To a proud father her performance was wonderful, but as I listened to the reaction of the audience, they agreed with me. God gave Kara a talent for singing and she has made it her life's work to share her music with others. There is no greater joy she could have given to me on Father's Day than singing from the heart on the very day set aside for showing love for her dad.

How do you think our Heavenly Father feels when He watches us using the talents and gifts, putting our heart into sharing it with others? He sees us working to develop the skills that bring joy to others. You know He is beaming from ear to ear when we use those skills for His Kingdom. He is watching every act of service, no matter how big or small, from His front row seat.

Scripture tells us that we don't get to Heaven by being good. Kara's performance on the stage, and yours in whatever charitable or helpful endeavor you choose, is not about personal gain or getting to Heaven. It is about our showing our faith by helping others. It is what we do because we are people of faith. We all are part of the family of God and we want to carry out God's plan for us to help others. It is all about sharing God's love with others.

Strive to please your Heavenly Father every day by doing things for others. It is a great gift on Father's Day or any day.

Scripture: *We love because He first loved us (1 John 4:19).*

Question: What gifts do you have that will please your Heavenly Father?

Prayer: We thank You for the talents You give us. We pray we will have the heart to use them to help others. Amen.

Topic: Honor Thy Mother
Special Day: Mother's Day

Honor Thy Mother

Mother's Day is the day we set aside to thank and honor our mothers. Restaurants will be full of families celebrating the special day with Mom. Flower shops and garden stores had a big day yesterday and moms will be receiving phone calls, greeting cards and gifts from their out-of-town children today. Moms have a special relationship with their children. They brought each child into the world and probably did a substantial share of changing diapers and preparing meals. They nursed injuries and drove the family taxi to ball games, school, and church activities. They live a life of sacrifice for their children. So on this special day we do our best to say thanks.

What kind of relationship did Jesus have with his mother? Mary brought the infant Jesus into the world. Could you imagine being the Mother of our Lord and Savior? Even before His birth Mary knew that Jesus had a divine purpose for being on earth. It was a lot to take in. *But Mary treasured up all these things and pondered them in her heart (Luke 2:19).*

Mary was special, too. Knowing she would give birth to the Son of God, Mary said, *My soul glorifies the Lord and my spirit rejoices in God my Savior, for he has been mindful of the humble state of his servant. From now on all generations will call me blessed, for the Mighty One has done great things for me—holy is his name (Luke 1:46-49).*

The relationship between Jesus and his mother is deep and vast. Jesus respected and loved his mother and He obeyed her every word. A great example of that is when Jesus and Mary attended a wedding at Cana. When they ran out of wine, Mary told Jesus to go with the servants to fix the wine situation. She was obviously aware of Jesus' power, and told the servants to *do whatever he tells you (John 2:5).* Jesus informed her that *my time had not yet come,* yet out of respect, he complied with her request. Jesus remained obedient to His parents in keeping with the fifth commandment. *Honor your father and your mother, that your days may be long upon the land which the Lord your God is giving you (Exodus 20:12).*

There are a few references to Mary accompanying Jesus in ministry. *After this he went down to Capernaum with his mother and brothers and his disciples. There they stayed for a few days (John 2:12).* It is clear Jesus, Mary, and Joseph must have lived a simple life because when Jesus returned to preach in His own hometown the people marvelled at His wisdom, power, and authority and said with some incredulity, *Is this not the carpenter, the son of Mary? (Mark 6:3).*

Jesus loved Mary so much that when he was being tortured on the cross he said, *woman, behold your son.* And then He said to the disciple, *Here is your mother,* to make sure Mary would be taken care of. *From that time on, this disciple took her into his home (John 19:27).*

Bruce Boyer

When Jesus said, *It is finished (John 19:30)*, it not only confirmed the end and completion of Jesus' earthly mission but Jesus also was telling Mary that His suffering was now over.

Mary gave birth to Jesus, and thanks to God's blessing, the mothers of today's world have given birth to other children in the Family of God. It doesn't get any more special than this. Enjoy your special relationship with your mom. And to all moms, happy Mother's Day.

Question: As children of God, how do we honor and celebrate our own mother's key role in our life?

Prayer: Dear Lord, today we celebrate the special life-giving, sacrificial role of mother's in our lives. We pray we will always honor our parents, as we honor You. Amen.

Topic: Easter/Promises Fulfilled
Holiday: Easter

Too Good to Be True?

When we see advertisements that seem too good to be true, they usually are. Read the fine print or research it further and you will find hidden costs – a deceptive tactic to get your business. The promises are empty. If the deal is unbelievable, it probably is.

So what about this claim that Jesus would die, be buried in a tomb, and come back to life three days later? If you hadn't read the book it sounds pretty far-fetched? No one had done this before. Is this even achievable? Jesus had promised this would happen and he kept his word. Still, people didn't understand what He was saying. Since He was the Messiah they thought He would never die, let alone need to come back to life. Even on the morning of the resurrection the 11 disciples didn't believe claims He had risen by the women who visited the empty tomb. Peter ran to the tomb to see for himself. It was true. Jesus had risen from the dead.

God always keeps his promises, In political campaigns candidates promise what they think you want to hear. The proof of their believability comes when they are in office. Their goal is to get elected. Their chances of being elected improved by making promises. All we can do is hope they are able to do what they promise.

In our relationship with God, the hope we seek is the hope for eternal life in heaven. God has promised believers eternal life. *The wages of sin is death, but the gift of God is eternal life in Christ Jesus our Lord (Romans 6:23).* Jesus communicated that directly to the people He met. *Jesus said to her, "I am the resurrection and the life. He who believes in me will live, even though he dies; and whoever lives and believes in me will never die" (John 11:25-26).* And God always keeps His promises.

Now for the price tag of the promise: Salvation is a *free* gift from God. That sounds too good to be true until you know the source — God himself. *If you confess with your mouth, "Jesus is Lord,"* **Instead of empty human promises, the empty tomb of the resurrected Jesus is our assurance of the truth.** *and believe in your heart that God raised him from the dead, you will be saved (Romans 10:9).*

Raising Jesus from the dead is something only God can do. It proves that Jesus is the Son of God. Not only was Jesus the Messiah (the "anointed one"), but the Savior of the world. The real pain and death Jesus suffered on the cross was what we, as sinners, deserved. And then, on the third day, Jesus overcame all of that. Jesus' resurrection was the victory over death for us, too. As a result, baptized believers can be free of sin as we seek to join Him in heaven.

It is a seemingly unbelievable story. But it is believable because God, the creator, is at the controls. There is nothing God can't do. When we believe in the resurrected Jesus we, too, can experience eternal life. Without God it is too good to be true, but with God all things are possible.

Question: What does the resurrection of Jesus Christ mean for you personally?

Scripture: *Jesus said, "Whoever believes and is baptized will be saved, but whoever does not believe will be condemned" (Mark 16:16).*

Prayer: Dear Lord, on this Easter Sunday we celebrate the resurrection of Your Son Jesus Christ. We thank You for the sacrifice of Your Son, so that we may have forgiveness of our sins and eternal life. Amen.

Topic: Resurrection
Holiday: Easter

Miracle Cure

There are times when a cancer subsides and, miraculously, no trace of it is found in the person. There are times when diseases seem to disappear overnight. Some of Jesus' most impressive miracles involve healing the sick. He helped the blind to see and the lame to walk. He raised Lazarus from the dead. God clearly has the power to heal.

So, with Jesus' life on the line, why didn't God perform a miracle and allow Jesus to come down from the cross? With Jesus enduring the scorn of mankind, blood streaming from his hands, feet and side, why didn't God stop the bleeding and allow Him to escape the cross?

But what would that have accomplished? Escaping the cross wouldn't have accomplished God's goal. God's goal was for Jesus to overcome death, and die for our sins. The miracle was not the coming down from the cross, but instead, raising Jesus from the dead three days later. Why? It was not Jesus who needed healing. It was --and still is -- *us* in need of God's healing. Jesus was -- and is -- perfect. We clearly are not. We needed Jesus to conquer death so that we could live, forgiven of our sins so we could enter God's Kingdom. This is the miracle accomplished because of God's love for us. And it does lead us to God's heavenly Kingdom. Jesus said, *I am the way, the truth and the life. No one comes to the father except through me (John 14:6).*

There are times when God heals our bodies. It gives us an opportunity to minister to others because of the additional time on earth God gives us. More important, however, is God's healing of our *souls.*

Don't be short-sighted as were the Romans. The Romans thought they accomplished that task of killing Jesus on that Friday noon. Mission accomplished? Not so fast: God used the Romans' cruel, cowardly act to set the stage for Jesus' victory over sin and death. Jesus died that day so that we could live. The resurrected Jesus lives, too. This is the miracle that we all need.

Scripture: *But our citizenship is in heaven. And we eagerly await a Savior from there, the Lord Jesus Christ, who by the power that enables him to bring everything under his control, will transform our lowly bodies that that they will be like his glorious body (Philippians 3: 20-21).*

Question: What does the resurrection mean to you?

Prayer: Dear Lord, the resurrection is a miracle, a victory over sin and death. You did that for us. We thank You for this sacrifice, so we can live. Amen.

Bruce Boyer

Topic: Resurrection
Holiday: Easter

He Is Not Here; He Has Risen

Have you marveled at the sleight of hand of an accomplished magician? Doves miraculously appear, coins disappear, only to reappear behind someone's ear in the audience? Swords are thrust through wooden boxes but the attractive lady inside the box is totally unharmed. How do they do that? Right in front of your eyes, seemingly miraculous things happen. Is that what happened on the morning of Jesus' resurrection? Was Jesus really unharmed on the cross of Calvary, the nails somehow missing his hands? Was it all a mirage? Or did Jesus endure everything to rise above it all?

After a long, sorrowful weekend, the people of Jerusalem were in need of some magic. Their Lord and Savior, who brought people back to life, helped lifelong cripples to walk, and healed the blind, had been whipped, beaten, and crucified right before their eyes. There is nothing fake about the punishment Jesus endured. Friday had been a dark day, with three hours of strange total darkness in midday. The earth shook and the giant temple curtain ripped from top to bottom at the very moment Jesus breathed his last breath. His seemingly lifeless body had been given to Joseph of Arimathea for burial in Joseph's family tomb. The hope of the world had died a terrible, painful death. Was it all over?

Then Sunday morning came. An earthquake shook the earth, and an angel rolled the several-ton stone away. Before first light, Mary and Mary Magdalene arrived at Jesus' tomb, walking into the open mouth of the cave. The angel greeted the two Marys with the comforting words, *He is not here; he has risen, just as he said (Matthew 28:6).* The angels instructed the women to go tell the disciples that Jesus was alive. As the women hurried from the tomb, Jesus met them and reassured them not to be afraid.

Remember Jesus' words to Martha and Mary at the time he raised Lazarus: *I am the resurrection and the life. He who believes in me will live, even though he dies; and whoever lives and believes in me will never die (John 11:25-26).* In this scriptural passage there is one more critical statement to make it meaningful for you and for me. The final words of this scriptural passage are *Do you believe this?* This is when it becomes personal, and is no longer a spectator event. How about you? *"Do you believe this"* is the deal maker for us.

You can buy books that explain how a magician's tricks work. They explain how to be deceptive in fooling the people. It can be done by anyone who diligently practices the craft. You can also buy books that explain the resurrection. This is not a trick, but instead is a demonstration of God's power and the fulfillment of promises. There is no amount of practice you can do to master a resurrection. It's God's work, only.

On Easter Sunday we celebrate the resurrection of our Lord Jesus Christ. He lives, so we can live too. *And Jesus Christ our Lord was shown to be the Son of God when God powerfully raised him from the dead by means of the Holy Spirit. Through Christ, God has given us the privilege and authority to tell Gentles everywhere what God has done for them, so that they will believe and obey him, bringing glory to his name (Romans 1:4-5).*

The resurrection completes Jesus' earthly ministry. From the cross Jesus said, *It is finished (John 19:30)*. It fulfills God's promises to us that Jesus is the Messiah. It demonstrates that Jesus overcame death and now lives. As people of faith, we, too, can live. Now it is up to us to tell others. Jesus told the two Marys to tell the disciples, and that Jesus would personally meet them ahead. He is waiting to personally meet us, too. Do you believe? If so, look forward to your wonderful encounter with the risen Christ. *He who believes in me will live (John 11:25)*. What a beautiful Easter sunrise.

Prayer: Dear Lord, on Easter Sunday we celebrate the resurrection of Your Son, Jesus Christ. He has risen, overcoming sin and death, defeating the devil, and fulfilling Your promise of eternal life. There is no greater gift. We thank You! We praise You! Amen.

Topic: Living a Christian Life
Season: Christmas

Mary Did You Know?

As parents, we don't know what the future holds for our kids. We bring a child into the world, do our best to provide a good Christian home, and hope and pray they will live out a purposeful life.

Can you image what it was like for Mary, the mother of Jesus? She had been told in a dream her son was special, and in the most humble settings, she gave birth to a beautiful baby boy.

God's plan for Jesus' life is musically presented in the inspirational Christmas anthem, "Mary Did You Know?" It speaks directly to the mother of Jesus Christ. What an awesome responsibility. Like any mother, Mary wanted the best for her child. In reality, her child wanted what is best for not only His mom, but for all mankind. As the song lyrics say to Mary, "This Child that you delivered will soon deliver you."

The lyrics continue, telling Mary when she kissed "your little Baby you kissed the face of God." Wow! Can you imagine what that would be like? I have tenderly kissed each of my children and grandchildren as I held them in my arms. The song concludes with the line, "The sleeping Child you're holding is the Great, I Am." The little baby in her arms is the Savior of the world.

So, how about you? You are a child of God, created in the image of God. You have been granted the gift of life to do good things in the name of Jesus Christ. Would your mom appreciate the person you have become? Would her heart be warmed by your kindness towards others, your love of all people, and your attempts to lead a Christian way of life? Does she know that you are a follower of Jesus? What thoughts of you will she treasure in her heart?

Jesus exceeded everything we could imagine, fulfilling every prophecy and creating the way for our eternal life. Mary couldn't have imagined the impact her son would have on the world, but she *treasured all these things, pondering them in her heart (Luke 2:19)*. Has your life exceeded the expectations of your mom? We all are a work in progress, but are you on the right path?

On Christmas Eve think about your role living the life God intended for you. Celebrate the birth of the Christ child and what it means for you. Then go out and seek to be the person God intended you to be. It will make your mom proud and it will honor your Heavenly Father.

Scripture: *But the angel said to her, "Do not be afraid, Mary; you have found favor with God. You will conceive and give birth to a son, and you are to call him Jesus. He will be great and will be called the Son of the Most High. The Lord God will give him the throne of his father David, and he will reign over Jacob's descendants forever; his kingdom will never end"* (Luke 1:30-33).

Question: What ways do you serve God that your mom would treasure in her heart?

Prayer: Dear Lord, we thank You for the gift of life. We pray we will honor You with what we do with our life. Amen.

Bruce Boyer

Topic: Sharing the Faith
Season: Christmas

Being Bold in the Faith

 Imagine yourself sitting down for a quick lunch at a mall food court. It seems to be more crowded than usual, but it is the Christmas season. A piano player is playing politically correct Christmas songs like "Jingle Bells" and "Here Comes Santa Claus." No one pays attention; it is just background music playing. Then it happens. As "Frosty the Snowman" finishes, a person belts out the first line of a familiar song. A few people take notice. Then, from across the food court another person stands up, singing the second line. That couldn't be a coincidence, so a few more people start to perk up. By the time a third singer joins in, it clearly gets the attention of every diner in the food court. Obviously, this was a flash mob singing one of the most inspirational songs ever written – the "Hallelujah Chorus" from Handel's <u>Messiah</u>. By the end of the song hundreds of people join in, including shoppers who were swept up in the spectacular musical expression of faith.

195

Could you image what it would be like to be dining in the middle of all the action? A minute ago you were minding your own business, drinking a cup of coffee, eating a slice of pizza, and trying to plan your Christmas shopping strategy. Then you are in the midst of one of the most powerful anthems. Your heart starts beating faster. "King of Kings and Lord of Lords; forever and ever. Hallelujah. Hallelujah."

Look at the surprised expression on the kids. They are thinking, "Adults don't generally step out of their comfort zone and do this. This must be something special."

Suddenly political correctness isn't important? "Jingle Bells" doesn't offend anyone, but it doesn't inspire either. Isn't it illegal to sing a Christian song in public? Can we get arrested for this? Do people even want to hear about Jesus Christ? They do! A YouTube link shows an astronomical number of "likes" of this mall food court scene. Ninety-seven percent of the people responding indicated they "liked" this performance, an overwhelming percentage considering people tend to speak up only if they have something negative to say.

Many people want the freedom to express their faith, but they are hesitant to take the first step. Some of those people joined in on the Hallelujah chorus at the food court. Others we can see humming it when watching the video clip. It becomes "safe" to express our faith as long as others are leading the way. We don't need conditions to be perfect in order to express our faith. Is the Great Commission only to be done in the safety of our sanctuaries at church – to people who already have a faith? The intent of the Great Commission is to share God's message to others who may not have heard it before -- like in the food court at the mall.

Look for opportunities to share your faith. Know that you are surrounded by supporters who will join in if someone takes the lead. You are not alone but *you* can be the person who steps up first. If someone didn't step up, the people at the mall food court would not have been inspired about the true meaning of the Christmas season.   Instead, they were moved by this expression of joy. We are joyful as we celebrate the birth of our Lord and Savior, Jesus Christ. Hallelujah. Hallelujah.

"*And He shall reign forever and ever*" are memorable words in the "Hallelujah Chorus." As fellow Christians, we want as many people as possible to be included in His Kingdom that lasts forever. If you want to make a difference in the world, you have to speak to those who don't – yet -- know of Christ's love for them.

Scripture: *Therefore, go and make disciples of all the nations, baptizing them in the name of the Father and the Son and the Holy Spirit. Teach these new disciples to obey all the commands I have given you. And be sure of this: I am with you always, even to the end of the age (Matthew 28:19).*

Question: How can you be bold in expressing your faith to those who need to know of God's love for them?

Prayer: Let us be bold, dear Lord. Take away our fears of being rejected because of our faith, and replace that fear with the satisfaction that we are encouraging others in their faith. Amen.

<u>Guest Author Stories</u>
<u>Featuring the YMCA's</u>
<u>Christian Mission</u>

Bob Kahle
Eric Ellsworth
Bob Warnock
Cliff Christian
Dan Doctor
Gray Stallworth
The Old Gray Goose
Larry Whittlesey
Bruce Ham
Rosemary Suess

Guest Author
Bob Kahle

Bob and Tina Kahle hold key leadership positions at their church and are involved in the home health care industry during their spare time. Tina currently works as a physical therapy assistant.

32 years in the camping profession for the YMCA has led Bob and his family to many regions of the country, and they have made friends throughout the world. Both have found the YMCA to be a great ministry and an opportunity to encourage and serve others. It has been a wonderful outlet to use his God-given talents while helping others learn and grow.

Bob has truly been an inspiration to me in how he visualizes faith lessons in everyday life, connecting the dots to make life experiences into a meaningful devotional story. His story, "Dreams of a 14-Year-Old Boy," is a true story about a youngster who transforms his life through a YMCA camp experience.

Topic: God Helps Us
Achieve Our Dreams

Dreams of a 14-Year-Old Boy

From the outside James was like many other 14-year-old boys, kind of awkward but trying his best to fit in. His vision of himself was clearly different than the image he presented to others. He spent a week at one of our trip camps. Seven days filled with hiking, canoeing, and rafting all while he made friends and shared stories. The stories children share on these trips are of their past experiences and their future dreams, and James was excellent at telling stories.

James dreamed of being a fighter pilot for the Air Force and described with great detail the posters on the wall of his bedroom, the books he had read, and the video games that helped him prepare for his future. His favorite activity was parkour or free-running, the activity where participants jump off things and run up walls: the martial art-like activities that one would normally just see in the movies or a pain-filled bloopers show. James told his new friends that the camp director had asked him to curtail his activity while on the trip as he didn't want other children to get hurt. James was filled with compassion for others and was eager to make friends so he was willing to oblige.

On the last day of camp I just happened to be talking with James' father, Mark, as James approached surrounded by his new friends. In awe of their new hero, the other boys peppered James' dad with questions: "Is James really a master at free-running? You really let him practice at your local park? Aren't you worried he will get hurt in the competitions? You've let him do this since he was 5?" The questions came fast and furious. Mark was silent. He just smiled and supported his son without saying a word, and eventually the boys walked away excited about the confirmation.

James' dad turned to me as the rush of adrenalin and testosterone walked away, and I noticed something was different about Mark. Mark had a small tear in his eye.

Mark told me that James was not a free-runner and never participated in parkour. Yes, he had dreams of being a fighter pilot for the Air Force and he had the posters in the bedroom to keep his dreams alive. But James walked with a limp not because of a parkour accident, but because he had scoliosis. In fact, the curvature of his spine was so severe that James wore a back brace 24 hours a day and 51 weeks of the year. His doctors viewed the camp experience as good therapy and allowed a week-long hiatus.

Mark chose this camp even though it was not close to his hometown area because he wanted James to be accepted for who he was and not be judged by his back brace. He got what he came for. For the first time in a long time James was just another 14-year-old boy with dreams and stories about who he was and who he would become.

How often do we wonder why we have challenges? Why our minds or bodies don't work as well as others? When we focus on our deficiencies we will be disappointed, but when we focus on the abilities God gives us we will overcome any challenge. We need to remember that God created us for a reason. In *Psalms 139:13-14*, David reminds us, *For you (God) created my inner most being; you knit me together in my mother's womb. I praise you because I am fearfully and wonderfully made; your works are wonderful, I know that full well.*

Bob Kahle
YMCA Fairview Lakes Camps, NJ

Guest Author
Eric Ellsworth

Eric Ellsworth is the President & CEO of the YMCA of Greater Indianapolis (Indiana). In a 40-year career, Eric is one of the YMCA directors most committed to help the Y continue maintain its Christian mission focus.

Eric has been a keynote speaker at five Christian Leadership Conferences and provided guitar and vocal music for 15 CLC's. He serves on the board for the US Mission Network, published the YMCA's Christian Emphasis newsletter, <u>Dunamis</u>, and served on the planning committee for several national "John 17:21" conferences. Eric recently affirmed that "Christ is doing powerful work through the YMCA, for His glory."

Eric has two stories in the book. The first, "A Modern Day Chrstmas Miracle," shows how God works through people to help others. "How Does Your Garden Grow," is a lesson in overcoming adversity.

Topic: With God All
Things Are Possible

A Modern Day Christmas Miracle

Each year the YMCA of Greater Indianapolis works with the Marine Corps to provide Christmas gifts to children in poverty in the city. This program has grown over its 15-year history from serving a few hundred children, to now serving more than 6,000.

This day is always such an inspiring one for the hundreds of volunteers who serve the children. The parents always seem so pleased and grateful to have something nice for their children for Christmas. The children are giddy with delight at the prospect of toys. You can see the light in their eyes!

In year 12, an unusually high number of families came out for the event. Even though most of the families pre-register, we always accept walk-ins after the pre-registrants are served. This particular year, however, the toys were running low.

When we saw that we were about to run out of gifts, the staff started making announcements for certain age groups and that we would soon be completely out.

But no one was leaving the line. Everyone was holding onto the hope that there would be enough for everyone.

Soon all the gifts were handed out, but there still were about 150 people in line.

A volunteer announced that we were out of toys completely, but still the people stayed in line – no one moved!

About that time, I could see some excitement around an open door at the side of the building. A volunteer ran up to announce that a man had driven up with another car full of toys and wanted to donate them. This man had been collecting toys at a local car dealership but had not been able to find a place to donate them.

Immediately, eight or 10 volunteers ran to the car with large boxes and began loading them with toys. First toys from the trunk and then the backseat and then the front seat were unloaded to restock the tables. We were back in business!!

We began the process again, passing out toys to children and families. As each family was being served it seemed more and more apparent that something remarkable was happening. Multiple toys were being given to each child and yet there were still more toys on the tables. Finally, every child and family was served, with toys still on the table.

We had witnessed a modern day Christmas miracle!

It was physically impossible for this car to have held enough toys to serve all the people standing in line. Yet every child and every family was served, leaving enough toys to serve even more.

Was it hope and belief that kept families in the line after they already knew that all the toys were gone?

Does this event remind you of the story of Jesus and the loaves and fishes?

The truth is that all things are possible with God. In this case, God decided to do a modern day Christmas miracle for these families.

I saw this with my own eyes, as did many that day, and we know what we saw. This kind of experience can only be explained with God.

Scripture: *So He commanded the multitude to sit down on the ground. And He took the seven and the fish and gave thanks, broke them and gave them to His disciples; and the disciples gave to the multitude. So they all ate and were filled, and they took up seven large baskets full of the fragments that were left. Now those who ate were four thousand men, besides women and children (Matthew 15:35-38).*

Question: Have you seen an act of God's mercy and grace in your life? Are you keeping your eyes open for the power of God's hand?

Prayer: Lord, help me to be aware of Your movement in my life. Please open my eyes, that I might see that You are still active in our world today. Amen!

Eric J. Ellsworth
President & CEO
YMCA of Greater Indianapolis, IN

Bruce Boyer

Topic: Overcoming
Adversity

How Does Your Garden Grow?

 Just this summer, my wife and I decided we would have our trees cut back in our yard. We were trying to get the grass to grow in the backyard because too much shade had not allowed the sun to provide its nourishment. The trees were overgrown and the yard had turned to bare dirt.

We pruned the trees way back and honestly, after the trimming, they looked barren. They looked like they would make a great home for some hungry vultures.

Then after just a few weeks we watched the first few leaves pop out from the branches. As they took shape, we noticed that the leaves were larger and healthier than we had ever seen them before. Not only that, everything around them, grass, bushes, flowers, all seemed more vibrant and colorful than we had ever remembered.

All I could think of was the previous year, which for me was full of trials and pruning in my work and personal life. Things were bad at work, performance and personnel issues, and my stress level was high. As a result, I had health issues. It just seemed that everything possible that could have gone wrong went wrong!!!

This caused me to think about the story of Job and the various trials he faced. Job lost almost everything he had, possessions, family, and health: everything except his life, and still, he did not forsake God.

Now, I can't in good conscience compare my trials to those of Job, but I can say that just like Job, since the trials stopped that following year, life has seemed more vibrant, exciting, fulfilling – perhaps more than ever before!

You see, the thing is, God is good and sometimes we need a good pruning so that we can be healthy again and be of greater use to others.

God taught me a great deal through these trials, and I can honestly say I am better for the pruning. <u>I am also glad it is in the rearview mirror!</u>

Scripture:	*Every branch in me that does not bear fruit, he takes away, and every branch that bears fruit, he prunes so that it may bear more fruit (John 15:2).*
Question:	Do you welcome trials and difficulties as an op portunity from God? Or do you run from hard ship with all your might?
Prayer:	Thank You God for the pruning times in our lives, which help us to grow spiritually. Thank You that, through all the trials of life, You will never leave us or forsake us. Take what You need from us to that our faith can be stronger, our actions more meaningful, and our dependence

Bruce Boyer

be more on You. You are not only the Great
Healer, but also the Great Pruner! Amen.

Eric J. Ellsworth
President & CEO
YMCA of Greater Indianapolis

Guest Author

Bob Warnock

Bob Warnock, a dedicated YMCA professional for 41 years, worked in senior management positions with the YMCAs of Los Angeles, Long Beach, and Whittier, California. He is an accomplished guitarist and song leader, playing informally with Cat Stevens, Chris Montez, Dick Van Dyke, members of the New Christy Minstrels, and the We Five.

He has volunteered extensively with the Walker Foundation for three decades to strengthen the Christian mission of the YMCA.

It was his fantastic idea to invite YMCA leaders to write a guest story for this book as a way of honoring the YMCA's Christian mission across the nation. Bob's story, "Hugging a Tree," talks about the awe and majesty youngsters experience when in the presence of God's creation here on earth.

Bruce Boyer

Topic: Experiencing
God's Majesty

Hugging a Tree

Early on in my YMCA journey I was a volunteer camp counselor with my local Y, which served the predominately white community of San Pedro, CA. One summer we shared a camp session with the Crenshaw Y, which served a predominately African American neighborhood. We formed cabin groups that were half white kids and half black. There was some nervousness and even discomfort when we off-loaded our San Pedro kids at the Crenshaw Y, assembled our cabin groups, and re-boarded the busses for the ride up to camp. Of course at camp we all bonded, and by the end of the week our session was an intercultural success. But that's not my story.

On the ride up we counselors did all the little group building tricks our directors had taught us: name games, songs, planning a skit or song for the opening night campfire, etc. Our goal was to begin forming our cabin families, one of the goals of which was to be that when we got off the bus my cabin group would do so together, and not run off in nine different directions. I almost succeeded.

One of my campers, a Crenshaw kid who was probably nine years old and whom I will call Jimmy since I have long since forgotten his real name, was the smallest and quietest of my boys, at least on the bus ride. Our cabin got off the bus as planned, but Jimmy's eyes got wide and he broke ranks, making a bee line for the nearest Ponderosa pine tree and giving it a great big (or as big as he was able) hug. So we have fifteen or so groups of ten kids heading towards the campfire circle, and me and my group following the smallest among us to a pine tree.

As I began to peel Jimmy from the tree I noticed another group of older boys heading our way. They were laughing. I hoped it wasn't at me for failing in my assigned bus ride task. One of the older boys, another Crenshaw Y kid, reached us first. He was yelling to Jimmy, "I told you so! You didn't believe me but I told you so!"

As the story unfolded, I learned that the older boy, Jimmy's brother, and been to camp the previous summer. He came home reporting among other things that there were trees in camp so big you couldn't wrap your arms around them. Jimmy didn't buy it. In their neighborhood trees grew up out of holes in the sidewalk and were smaller than the street light poles. At camp there are no light poles, and trees older than our great-great-grandparents grow up out of the mountain.

I have forgotten much of what happened that week; it was 50 years ago after all. But I'll never forget Jimmy and his wonder, awe, and delight at meeting nature in a way that most of us take for granted.

I have come to believe that if we choose to take His hand, God will guide us through life day to day. In my heart I have no doubt that God brought Jimmy, me, and that tree together right there and then for His own purpose. I wish I knew where Jimmy is today. Wherever he is, I'm certain he's a better man for that childhood experience. I can also report that the trees in the Crenshaw district and bigger and better now, too.

Scripture: *Splendor and majesty are before him; strength and glory are in his sanctuary (Psalm 96:6).*

Question: How have you been awed when seeing the majesty of God's creation?

Prayer: Dear Lord, may every inner-city Jimmy in our world have a tree experience. May he know God's creation first-hand. May he bloom where he is planted and be a joy and a blessing to those who surround him.. Amen.

Bob Warnock
Los Angeles, CA

Guest Author

Cliff Christian

Cliff Christian is the spiritual life director for YMCA Blue Ridge Assembly, in Black Mountain, NC. He has 25 years of experience in ordained ministry, serving as a pastor, pastoral counselor, chaplin and missions coordinator. As part of his role at Blue Ridge, he coordinates the annual Blue Ridge Christian Leadership Conference.

Throughout his rewarding career his heart has been in social ministry with Micah 6:8 as his guiding principle: *What does the Lord require of you but to act justly, love kindness and walk with humility before your Lord.*

In 2007 Cliff began the Timothy Project, which engages young people in transformational Christian service. Volunteers in this program have provided over 100,000 hours of service throughout the southeastern United States.

Bruce Boyer

Topic: Using God's
Gifts in Service

Let Your Life Speak

Several years ago, I attended a college conference as part of my service leadership work. The theme of that conference was taken from Parker Palmer's classic book, <u>Let Your Life Speak</u> (John Wiley and Sons, Inc. 2000). The book is a study in encouraging the reader to find his or her true purpose in life. It begs the question, "What is my true vocation?" For this reason, it is a very popular book with young people as they are considering their life's work. I have found the question to be relevant for all of us, regardless of age. Now much older than a college student, I have come to believe that any true vocation must involve service to others. Frederick Buechner defines vocation as "The place where your deep gladness meets the world's deep need."

I was once invited to go on a retreat to a Catholic monastery. Well, I am Baptist and was not so sure about that. However, I trusted the person who invited me, and so I went along. I am so glad I did. This particular monastery had a business enterprise raising chickens and selling eggs to supermarkets. It was a big business! I would see the brothers in their robes for worship services, and then in jeans and flannel shirts working the farm. One brother gave me a tour of the farm. I asked him how long he had been a monk. He thought for a minute and said, "Next year will be 50 years." I was amazed. He then showed me what he did each day on the farm. His job was to mix the feed for the chickens. He spoke of it with great excitement! I had to ask him how long he had been doing this. He replied, "About 15 years." I was amazed again and asked how he could still have so much energy and excitement around such a task? He said something I have obviously never forgotten. "You can do anything when you realize you have a vocation." You see, his real vocation wasn't anything about chickens. His vocation was that of a monk and follower of Jesus, and his joy flowed from that reality.

Within each of us, God has planted seeds of faith, courage, skills, and abilities. Our job is to pay attention. Our former pastor at each baptism said these words: "You are a child of God and God takes great delight in you, and God has given you all the gifts you need to become the person He intended you to be." So…why wait?

LET your life speak. Your true self wants to be further revealed. We catch glimpses in the things we do and those "ah ha" moments. And in those times when we find ourselves to be smarter or stronger or braver than we thought we were.

Let YOUR life speak. No one can tell you what God has in store for you. You have the freedom to listen to your own life.

Let your LIFE speak. A seminary professor taught me that talk can be cheap. He said, "Pay attention to what people do, not what they say they will do." I think one of the greatest compliments that a person can receive is that he or she is genuine.

Let your life SPEAK. What is the language of your life? What speaks to you? What are your interests and the things you enjoy? My wife has taught in a school's gifted program. It is an interesting designation because we actually all are gifted in something. Some of her most satisfying work has been in identifying kids who were not thought to be gifted, only to find they just needed an opportunity!

Palmer writes, "Our deepest calling is to grow into our own authentic selfhood, whether or not it conforms to some image of what we ought to be." Let your life speak, and in the process you will make a difference in you and in the world.

Scripture: *"The Spirit of the Lord is on me, because he has anointed me to proclaim good news to the poor. He has sent me to proclaim freedom for the prisoners and recovery of sight for the blind, to set the oppressed free, to proclaim the year of the Lord's favor (Luke 4:18-19).*

Prayer: Lord Jesus, as you have revealed God the Father to us, your life has spoken grace, truth, power and above all, love. Help us in our journeys toward wholeness with the courage to live authentic lives. Amen.

Cliff Christian
Spiritual Life Director
YMCA Blue Ridge Assembly, NC

Guest Author

Terra Lynn Dearth

Terra Lynn Dearth is the national Director of the YMCA Christian Leadership Conferences/Rags & Leathers program. She is employed by the YMCA of Greater Long Beach, California, on behalf of the CJ, Carrie D. and R. Howard Walker Foundation. Terra Lynn has administered Christian Leadership conferences and the Rags & Leathers programs nationally since 1980. During that 36-year time period 15 different YMCAs have hosted regional conferences to train Y staff to carry out its Christian mission. The conferences have attracted 50,000 participants who have influenced more than 20 million lives for Christ back at their home YMCAs. Terra Lynn facilitates a great ministry that strengthens the faith of believers and plants seeds for Christ.

Her story, "How God Can Turn Tragedy Into Something Good," tells how the Walker Foundation was created in the wake of a tragedy. And we know that in all things God works for the good of those who love him, who have been called according to his purpose (Romans 8:28). Through the efforts of Terra Lynn and the Walker Foundation, the YMCA movement has a much stronger Christian mission.

Bruce Boyer

Topic: Turning Tragedy
into Victory

How God Can Turn
Tragedy into Something Good

*You intended to harm me, but God intended
it for good to accomplish what is now
being done, the saving of many
lives (Genesis 50:20).*

Life is full of twists and turns. Often bad things happen to good people. But somehow God can find the good in some of the most tragic situations. One of those situations happened to 22-year-old Howard Walker. Howard was working on a family project. He was at the bottom of a large ditch, with his brother operating a backhoe above. Sensing an impending collapse of the ditch wall, his brother yelled "Run!" Howard quickly responded, but ran the wrong way and was buried by a landslide. Life was cut short that September, 1973 day for young Howard, who was nearing the prime of his life.

Howard was the oldest of four brothers of a family firmly committed to the Lord. Some of their Christian commitment is expressed

219

through the Young Men's Christian Association, specifically the YMCA of Greater Long Beach. All the brothers enjoyed YMCA resident Camp Oakes, and had worked as volunteer counselors at the camp. Prior to the accident, Howard's brother, Dan, was a counselor in a trip program. Ken, Howard and Dan's father, was surprised the trip program was largely lacking in its Christian emphasis. There was no grace before meals out on the trail, and no devotions. God was left out of that camp experience. The family was disappointed that an organization founded as a Bible study organization (London, England, 1844) had lost its Christian focus. Perhaps not everywhere, but it was lacking at YMCA Camp Oakes.

Upon Howard's death, Ken met with YMCA leaders to determine how memorial funds could be used to help the YMCA. The decision was made to use the contributions to fund a weekend training event for Camp Oakes staff. The goal was to help camp staff better understand how to put Christian emphasis in their summer programs. The first Christian Leadership Conference was held in 1974, with approximately 150 attending.

God turned that one-time conference into an ongoing effort to motivate and enable Y staff in the Christian mission. Within a few years conferences were held nationwide, attracting not only resident camp staff, but also paid and volunteer leaders in all aspects of the Y. Conference attendees are offered a Bible inscribed with Howard's signature and highlighting Psalms 25:4-5, which says: *Show me your ways, LORD, teach me your paths. Guide me in your truth and teach me, for you are God my Savior, and my hope is in you all day long.* Conference attendees also receive C in the YMCA, a devotional book to use in their home Y's in addition to an inspirational weekend to motivate them in their faith.

Christian Leadership Conferences have become the grassroots strength for the YMCA's Christian mission, have helped better train and enhance the personal lives of over 50,000 leaders, and touched over 20,000,000 lives throughout the U.S.

Howard's tragic death was a blow to a strong Christian family fully invested with the YMCA in Long Beach. God truly had made something very good happen from that tragedy. The Walker family's commitment to help the YMCA carry out its Christian mission has influenced the YMCA movement nationwide. God can do the same in your life if you dedicate your life to serving our Lord, Jesus Christ.

Terra Lynn Dearth
National Director
YMCA Christian Leadership
Conferences/Rag & Leathers Program
Long Beach, CA

Guest Author
Dan Doctor

Each year Dan travels extensively throughout the United States as a representative of the Walker Foundation, which provides support for YMCA Christian Leadership conferences nationwide. Dan provides motivational leadership to a dozen or more CLC's each year as a keynote speaker, worship leader, and foundation representative. Dan is a school administrator in Lockport, New York. He grew up at the Lockport YMCA's Camp Kenan. When you read his story, "He Made a Promise," you will understand Dan's commitment to serving the Lord.

Bruce Boyer

Topic: Honoring
Our Promise

He Made a Promise

A young man growing up in the Garden Street apartments graduated from high school. Determined to be successful, he followed his dream and headed off to New York City to study at Fashion Institute of Technology, an internationally recognized college for design, fashion, art, communications, and business. One year into his studies, the young man was stricken with an illness that devastated his family and baffled physicians.

This young man had come home for a spring break and met up with his friends to have dinner and catch a movie. After the eventful evening, the young man returned home with a massive headache. The pain shot rapidly across his head, forcing his eyes to stay shut tight. His mother, hearing the young man moan from the pain, entered his room to investigate the noise coming from within the bedroom. As she entered, she found her son lying on the bed, tears streaming down his face from the pain pounding within his head. He informed her of his condition. She immediately went to the bathroom down the hall and brought back a washcloth that she had run under cold water, placing it on his head to ease the pain. As she held her child in her arms, she did what she knew best, and that was to pray. She knew God answered prayers. After seeing her child still struggling with the pain, they both agreed he should go to the emergency room. They waited patiently for a taxi to arrive at the lower town apartments to transport to the local hospital.

The young man and his mother sat in the waiting room. When they called his name he could barely stand, let alone walk to the triage station. As they checked his blood pressure, they realized it was life-threatening. The medical technicians immediately rushed him into a room and began treatment. The young man drifted in and out of consciousness. After stabilizing his vitals, he was then transferred to a nearby hospital where the family physician practiced and was placed into ICU. In the wee hours of the morning, the young man was awakened by an intense pounding in his chest. As he peered down at his hospital gown, he could see his chest rising and falling rapidly. The machines that were attached to him began to beep uncontrollably and nurses flooded the room. The young man became violently ill and nurses administered a nitroglycerin tablet under his tongue. He settled and drifted off to sleep. In the morning he was informed he gave the ICU unit a scare. His doctor arrived and informed his mother he would be transferred to a third hospital that specialized in medical oncology and would be admitted into the ICU until further notice.

Six weeks passed in the new facility. Physicians and nurses worked around the clock studying, prodding and probing the young man. On the seventh week of hospitalization, the young man was diagnosed with phaeochromocytoma; a neuroendocrine tumor in the medulla of the adrenal glands. They would have to perform surgery on this 19-year-old. Fighting back tears, the young man thought the worst.

Days before surgery the young man made a promise;

"God, I know you can hear me. You know everything about me. Lord I need your help. I am scared. I don't want to die. Please let me wake up from this surgery. I have so much to do. God, if you heal me, I will serve you and do what you want me to do. Please God I need you."

That young man is me. Today I am cancer free, to God be the glory, and have been called into ministry. I have been graciously asked to be a part of a Christian Leadership Team through the Walker Family of Long Beach, California, to speak around the country spreading the good news of my faith and the goodness of Jesus at YMCA Christian Leadership Conferences around the world, which train day and resident camp leaders, child care workers, YMCA staff, and volunteers on how to implement the YMCA Rag/Leather Program, the implementation of Christian values in the YMCA, devotions, prayer, chapel, values education, and much more.

I made a promise.

Daniel W. Doctor
Lockport, NY

Guest Author

Gray Stallworth

Gray Stallworth is recently retired as Executive Director of the Greenwood Family YMCA, in Greenwood, South Carolina, after a 36 year career. He worked for YMCAs in North and South Carolina.

For many years Gray directed the largest YMCA Christian Leadership Conference in the nation, held at Blue Ridge Assembly (Black Mountain, NC) and has been a Walker Foundation volunteer and YMCA prayer warrior for decades. He is well known for portraying the character of George Williams, the founder of the YMCA in London, England (1844). Gray's story, "Etched on My Heart," presents a personal, true story of keeping God close to your heart.

Bruce Boyer

Topic: Keeping God
Close to Your Heart

Etched on My Heart

When I was a teenager, a lot of my friends began to wear a medallion around their necks. So, one day my dad brought me a medallion from a trip he had taken. I thought it was pretty cool at the time. I wore the chain very low on my chest, right over my heart. On the top side, there was a depiction of Christ's head. The verse around the edge was a favorite verse of mine while growing up. *I can do all things through Christ who strengthens me (Philippians 4:13).*

On the reverse side was a picture of an open Bible. The verse around the edge was from *Romans 8:31" If God be for us, who can be against us?*

When I was 16, my father had a fatal heart attack. It was a time of confusion for me. I couldn't always understand why this had happened. But even after dad's death, I wore that medallion and remembered that it was a gift from him. I often looked at the medallion and would repeat those verses again and again.

After graduating from college, getting married, and beginning a career, I found that medallion one day. I looked at it carefully and discovered something that I will never forget. On the reverse side of the medallion, the scripture that was once there was almost totally worn off. You could hardly read it. That verse that was once there was now etched permanently on my heart. My parents helped etch many verses on my heart, and this one will always have special meaning for me.

Scripture: *Then he spoke to the children of Israel, saying: "When your children ask their fathers in time to come, saying, 'What [are] these stones?' "then you shall let your children know, saying, 'Israel crossed over this Jordan on dry land'; "for the LORD your God dried up the waters of the Jordan be fore you until you had crossed over, as the LORD your God did to the Red Sea, which He dried up before us until we had crossed over (Joshua 4:21-23 NKJV).*

Question: Are you intentionally teaching about God's work in your life? Through traditions or gifts or special dates, do you specifically work to keep memories of His presence and His faithfulness alive in your family?

Prayer: Dear Heavenly Father, I pray that the lessons taught to me as a child will always be etched on my heart. I pray that Your Word will always remain with me. In Your Son's name I pray. Amen.

Gray Stallworth
Retired Executive Director
Greenwood YMCA
Greenwood, NC

Guest Author

The Old Gray Goose

The Old Gray Goose is a retired YMCA professional, having worked for the YMCA his entire adult life. His stories and persona are legendary. He has worked for the YMCA in Worchester, Mass., and Lockport, NY.

Goose was my mentor during my teenage years when I was a counselor at YMCA Camp Kenan. My previous book, 24/7 – Stories of Faith From Everyday Life, was dedicated to him. Goose was a major influence in my selecting the YMCA as a career. "Conrad the Shoemaker" is a devotional story Goose has told at YMCA camp.

Topic: Serving God
by Serving Others

Conrad the Shoemaker

Once there was a shoemaker named Conrad. And around Christmastime he had been reading the story of the birth of Jesus. He thought he would make a gift for the baby Jesus, so he made a pair of shoes that were white, the best pair of shoes he had ever made.

Well, he went home that night, and while he slept, he had a dream. He had a dream that on the next day God was going to come and visit him in his shoemaker shop.

So he rushed down to his shoemaker shop early in the day and took a broom to it, and then he sat down and began to repair shoes. Early in the morning a young man came in, and he walked over to where Conrad was fixing shoes.

"Sir, I have some shoes that need fixing."

"Oh, that's alright," Conrad said. "Give them to me."

"I'm afraid you don't understand. You see, the shoes that need fixing are on my feet."

"Oh, why that's alright, sure, no problem. Sit down, take them off and I'll repair them while you wait."

"Uh … well, I'm afraid you still don't understand. I don't have any money to pay you."

"Oh, that's alright. Sit down, take your shoes off; I'll fix them. When you get the money, you bring it in. After all, it's Christmas. "

So the man sat down and took off his shoes, and the two began talking. Conrad fixed his shoes and the young man went on his way, saying "Goodbye, friend," and Conrad waited. After all, God was going to visit him that day.

It became early afternoon, and Conrad was looking out his front window as it began to snow. He saw an old woman go by. She had in one arm a bag of groceries and in the other arm she had some Christmas presents. Just as she got in front of Conrad's shop, she must have slipped on a wet piece of snow, and her bags and boxes and everything went all over. Conrad rushed out and helped her up and into his shop, sitting her down by his stove. And then he went out and picked up all the groceries and presents and gave the woman some coffee to warm her soul. And they began talking. After she was all better again, Conrad even called a cab to take her home. "Goodbye, friend," she said as she left. After she left, Conrad waited and waited, for after all, God was to come and visit him that day.

It became late afternoon. Conrad thought he heard something like the voice of a child, and Conrad went out. There in the entryway, was a little girl, maybe two or three years old. She had no coat on and was lost. Conrad picked her up and made some hot chocolate for her. After she got warm, she remembered where she lived, only she had no phone. Conrad, he didn't know why he did it, but he reached onto the shelf and took down the special pair of shoes that he had made for Jesus. He put them on the little girl's feet and said, "I'm going to take you home." And he took the little girl because she lived near to Conrad's shop, and then he rushed back and opened up his shop. He waited and waited into the night.

He closed his shop, went home, and made something to eat, and he was sort of saying to himself, "I don't even know why I believed there was a God. He said he was going to come and visit me today and he didn't."

Then he heard a voice that said, "Conrad. Conrad. How foolish you are. Three times I came to visit you this day and you did not know me. I was the young man, I was the old woman, and I was the little girl. I came to your shop three times today, and you did not know me."

Scripture: *For I was hungry and you gave me something to eat, I was thirsty and you gave me something to drink, I was a stranger and you invited me in, I needed clothes and you clothed me, I was sick and you looked after me, I was in prison and you came to visit me. Then the righteous will answer him, 'Lord, when did we see you hungry and feed you, or thirsty and give you something to drink? When did we see you a stranger and invite you in, or needing clothes and clothe you? When did we see you sick or in prison and go to visit you?' The King will reply, 'Truly I tell you, whatever you did for one of the least of these brothers and sisters of mine, you did for me' (Matthew 25:35-40).*

Question: Think of an example of a time when you helped a complete stranger. Did you realize you were serving Jesus?

Prayer: Heavenly Father, You are present in the needy people: those who are hungry, the homeless, and those needing clothing. When we serve the needy we are serving You. Amen.

This is not an original story. It is copied with permission from Devotions, Morning Thoughts, & Other Camp Stories, a collection of stories told by The Old Gray Goose. Goose has told these stories for generations at YMCA Camp Kenan, a camp operated by the Lockport (N.Y.) YMCA. I attended this camp as a youth and then as a counselor for many years.

Guest Author

Larry Whittlesey

Larry Whittlesey is the National Director of the US Mission Network based in Portland, Oregon. The first time Larry set foot in the YMCA was to be the Executive Director of the US Mission Network, an organization that supports the Christian mission of the YMCA. He has taken the YMCA by storm to provide excellent direction to the mission movement of the YMCA.

Larry has been in the pastoral ministry for 38 years and is a former National Event Director for Promise Keepers. With his role with the US Mission Network he now travels around the country helping to promote the Christian mission of the YMCA. His passion continues to be to help Christians understand the joy of service and apply the truths of scripture to their daily lives.

His story in this devotional book, "Standing on Holy Ground," talks about the preparation, respect, and honor of when we get to stand on Holy Ground, in the presence of the Heavenly Father.

Topic: Preparation

Standing On Holy Ground

It's one of the sites everyone who visits Washington, D.C., should take in! While it's not located adjacent to the White House and the Capitol Building like so many other monuments, it is perhaps the most impressive site of them all.

Located across the Potomac River just west of the Lincoln Memorial is Arlington Cemetery, the final resting place for thousands of U.S. military personnel, patriots, and Presidents. It's an impressive place, but there's one spot in Arlington that is an absolutely "must see" destination: the Tomb of the Unknown Soldier.

The Tomb itself is nothing spectacular. No one leaves the Tomb overly impressed with the grandeur of the architecture. But they do leave incredibly moved by what they see there! What they see is a remarkable tribute to those who have so valiantly fought for our freedom.

The guards at the Tomb are one of the most elite units in the U.S. military. Soldiers from the Army's 3rd Infantry Regiment (The Old Guard) have that task. These dedicated soldiers guard the Tomb 24 hours a day, 365 days a year. They pace 21 steps across the front of the tomb, pause for 21 seconds, then do an about face and march 21 steps back to their starting position, repeating the process without interruption. A 21-gun salute is the highest honor given in the military, thus explaining the soldier's routine.

These soldiers commit two years of their lives to this process, living in barracks under the Tomb. They spend an average of 5 hours per day just getting their uniforms ready.

To the men and women who are dedicated to this work, what they do is not a mere show. It is a charge of honor. The steady rhythmic step in rain, sleet, snow, hail, heat and cold must be uninterrupted. To these men the continuity of this post is the key to the honor and respect shown to these honored dead.

Seeing this in person is a truly moving experience. It's obvious that these soldiers take this responsibility and privilege seriously. This is not some trivial pursuit: it is worthy of their very best!

As God's children, we have all been given access to an even greater responsibility and privilege. God has given us all direct access to Him. Through His Word and prayer He invites us to enter into His presence. Unfortunately, too often we either don't take advantage of that opportunity, or we come unprepared, distracted. We invest too little time or thought into the process.

When we come into God's presence we are "standing on holy ground." We've been invited to participate in something that is truly eternal. The significance of that opportunity cannot be overstated. God deserves our best, our full attention, and our commitment to the experience when we spend time with Him! Perhaps these soldiers can teach us all a lesson about preparation, respect, and honor!

Scripture: *"What message does my Lord have for his servant?" The commander of the Lord's army replied, "Take off your sandals, for the place where you are standing is holy" (Joshua 5:14b-15).*

Question: Are you preparing yourself to stand on "holy ground" or just checking off the blanks in your time alone with God?

Prayer: Father, please help me to take full advantage of the privilege You have given me to stand in Your presence. May I never take it for granted the op portunity You have given me to be in a personal relationship with You!

Larry Whittlesey
National Director
US Mission Network
Portland, OR

Guest Author
Bruce Ham

Bruce Ham is the Chief Development Officer, YMCA of the Triangle Area (NC). He has dedicated his entire 31-year career to the
YMCA in the Raleigh, NC area. Bruce has written his own book,
Laughter Tears and Braids, which reveals the struggle of a husband and wife raising three daughters as his wife, Lisa, was battling
cancer. Bruce's story in this book, "What Counts the Most," is
told through the eyes of his three daughters. Bruce is a highly motivational YMCA leader with a tender, but powerful message about
the importance of appreciating the little things of family life.

Topic: Small Things
Count

What Counts the Most

It may not be the big things in life that you're most remembered for. Three years ago today, my wife died peacefully at Duke Medical Center at the age of 39 from colon cancer. Last night, I asked my three daughters what they most remembered about Mom.
It wasn't her leadership in the community or the fact that she spearheaded the effort to build their new school. It wasn't her accomplishments at the Junior League or the vision she shared on the church building committee. What they remembered most were the small things.

"Mom always wanted to shop at Harold's at the mall. As soon as she was finished shopping, she'd take us to the candy store right by the escalators. I looked forward to that every time!"

Sweet memories. Sweet, sweet memories.

They recalled that she constantly drank diet Dr. Pepper and that her fingernails were impeccable. My oldest daughter remembered that she once got addicted to Afrin nose spray - wouldn't leave the house without it!

She'd only listen to one type of music at a time - winter often brought country, the summer was pop. You didn't even think about changing the Christmas station from November 1st on.

She was a stickler for tradition - chili and cornbread on Christmas Eve and the song "Take Me Home, Country Roads" as we drove over the mountain to our annual August getaway in West Virginia.

One of the things that they miss the most is her back scratches. "Dad, you don't have fingernails. Mom scratched. You give a nub rub."

Instead of trying to change the world, maybe I should just grow out my fingernails and take more visits to the candy store. In the end, maybe that's what counts the most.

Scripture: *But God chose the foolish things of the world to shame the wise; God chose the weak things of the world to shame the strong (1 Corinthians 1:27).*

Question: Are we chasing the foolish and weak things of the world or are we spending time on the things that count the most?

Prayer: Heavenly Father, sometimes we get so involved with the big tasks we don't realize the impact we have on people by just being ourselves, and doing the little things that make people happy. Let us be an example to others in everything we do. Amen.

Bruce Ham
Chief Development Officer
YMCA of the Triangle Area, NC

Guest Author

Rosemary Suess

Rosemary Suess is the Executive Director of the Jerry Long Family YMCA, the largest branch of the YMCA of Northwest North Carolina. Over her 20-year career she worked professionally at YMCAs in Kings Mountain and Charlotte, NC, New Orleans, LA, Kernersville, NC and now at the Jerry Long Branch in Winston-Salem, NC. She has led workshops for numerous Christian Leadership Conferences and serves on the planning committee for the Blue Ridge Assembly CLC.

When I retired from the workforce, Rosemary's commitment to her personal faith and the YMCA's Christian mission re-kindled my enthusiasm for volunteering at the YMCA I once directed. She is one of the best there is at directing a mission-focused YMCA, as evidenced by her personal goal to "share the Gospel of Jesus Christ through the YMCA." Rosemary's story, "The Trinity," talks about her earthly father who had different roles during various stages of her life, just as the Trinity of our Heavenly Father does the same for each of us.

Bruce Boyer

Topic: The Trinity
The Trinity
Genesis 1:26: "Let us make man in our image...." From the beginning, man was made in the image of the Trinity.

I envision my earthly father in three different physical states:
Youthful Dad as my father while growing up, Aging Dad as my
mentor as an adult, and Passing Dad as a mere shell of the man as
his soul left this world.

I was blessed with a charmed upbringing, at least in my eyes. With
one brother and three sisters, we had plenty of company ALL OF
THE TIME. Youthful Dad worked and Mom stayed home as was
traditional in those days. Youthful Dad still managed to help with
homework, come to games and school plays whenever possible,
and manage the glorious two-week summer vacations at the beach.
Youthful Dad was a father who always had a presence, even when
not physically there. God the Father is always with me and always
has a presence.

As I moved into adulthood, Aging Dad still had a presence, although not necessarily physically, as I had my own home and family. I heard his voice when making decisions, I called on him in
times of trouble, and I celebrated with him in times of joy. Aging
Dad was my mentor whom I wanted to please. God the Son is
always with me and I want to please Him.

Touchpoints of Faith

My father passed on April 22nd, 2015, after succumbing to stomach and esophagus cancer. I had the honor and privilege to spend the last night of his life with him here on earth. During that time, Dad clearly began his passing; speaking to those unseen "toggling", if you will, between this world and the next. My first thought was hallucinations due to medications. However, Dad was not on anything but a little morphine for pain. It was an affirmation of my faith and an enlightening experience which sounds strange but is the honest truth. Passing Dad reaffirmed the ultimate reason we are here on earth: this life is temporary so make the most of each day, spread the Good News, and glorify the Lord. God the Holy Spirit is always with me.

The Lord provides us an earthly father to provide for many earthly needs. My earthly father was my guide in many ways. The Heavenly Father is the ultimate guide in the form of the Trinity; God the Father, God the Son, God the Holy Spirit. Do you trust God the way you trust your earthly father? Do you allow him to guide you, mentor you, and show you what's most important in this temporary life in order to prepare for the everlasting life to follow?

Scripture: *I have set before you life and death, blessing and curse. Therefore choose life, that you and your offspring may live, loving the LORD your God, obeying his voice and holding fast to him, for he is your life and length of days, that you may dwell in the land that the LORD swore to your fathers, to Abraham, to Isaac, and to Jacob, to give them (Deuteronomy 30:19-20).*

Prayer: Father God, I know Your spirit dwells within me. I pray that I walk daily with this knowledge and shine with Your presence to all.

Rosemary Suess, Executive Director
Jerry Long Family YMCA
YMCA of Northwest North Carolina

Bible Study Section

for Additional Study

The stories in this section contain many more
Bible references than other stories in this book.

Topic: 10 Commandments

Are 9 out of 10 Enough?

Any baseball player would love to get on base 9 out of 10 times. A quarterback would make the Hall of Fame if he could complete 90 percent of his passes as would a basketball player shooting that kind of field goal percentage. In most school systems 90 percent is an A. But, are 9 out of 10 enough?

The Lord gave Moses the 10 Commandments on Mt. Sinai, etching them in stone to emphasize their permanence. The first four commandments pertain to our relationship with God, while the remaining six commandments address how the faithful relate to each other.

God asks us to keep all 10 Commandments. We can't ignore one and think keeping the other 9 are good enough. We don't live a Godly life by choosing which commandments are convenient for us and ignoring others. Since the 10 Commandments define sin, we cannot choose to set any aside.

It is not an easy task. The pace and pressures of life encourage us to place objects and obsessions ahead of God. We are tempted to covet things others have. We're not always truthful and when we are upset, we are tempted to blame God by using His name dishonorably. Is it OK to slander God's name when you are mad – the same name you call on when you are in trouble and need something?

So, how are you doing on withstanding the temptations of life? For Godly people, some commandments are not much of a challenge. But, can you go 10 for 10? How committed are you on setting aside God's Holy Day? If God rested on the seventh day, who are you to ignore this Holy Day? By what authority do you justify breaking any of God's commandments? Jesus came to us to take away all our sins so that we can be right with God.

Why do we seek to keep the 10 Commandments? We do not keep the 10 Commandments in order to be saved. We keep them because we are saved. May your commitment to the Lord be etched in stone as an eternal covenant with a loving God.

A brief summary of the intent of the 10 Commandments:

I. Loyalty – demonstrating our loyalty by having no other Gods (Exodus 20:2-3).

II. Worship – God prohibits worship of idols (Exodus 20:4-6).

III.Reverence – God instructs us to respect His holy name and not use it in vain (Exodus 20:7).

IV. Sanctification and worship - Remember the Sabbath and set it apart for Holy purposes to draw near to Him (Exodus 20:8-11).

V. Respect for parental authority – show love for our parents by honoring them (Exodus 20:12).

VI. Respect for human life – demonstrate love, not hatred, towards others (Exodus 20:13).

VII. Purity in relationships – demonstrate pure love by not committing adultery (Exodus 20:14).

VIII. Honesty – God instructs us not to steal *(Exodus 20:15).*

IX. Truthfulness – God instructs us not to lie or deceive others *(Exodus 20:16).*

X. Contentment – God instructs us not to covet because He knows it can entrap us into greater sins *(Exodus 20:17).*

Question: What commandments are most difficult for you to keep? How do you combat the temptation to think that keeping most of them is enough?

Prayer: Heavenly Father, the 10 Commandments date back to the time of Moses, yet are as relevant today as they were then. They teach us how to be loyal and respectful. They teach us honesty and truthfulness. They encourage us to be content with what we have, and to worship You rather than the objects of our dreams. They teach us to be pure in our relationships with others. Help us to be 10 for 10 on our efforts to keep Your commandments. Amen.

Bruce Boyer

Topic: Direction

Dear Amy

 There are a few sections of the daily paper that I read on a regular basis. One of those sections I find interesting is the advice column.

Why do we want to read about other people's problems? I don't revel in other people's struggles, although in daily life, a goal of mine is to provide support to friends and family whenever I can. When reading the advice column, I want to see if God agrees with the solution suggested by the columnist. I hope that the columnist's thoughts and faith-based answers will be the same. God has the answers to our problems today. That is the advice we should seek.

Most of the problems in the newspaper are about relationships. Often, the person writing for advice feels they are right and are trying to find someone who publically agrees with them. If the columnist backs up their position perhaps they can either discretely or maybe overtly reveal the now-national discussion about their once private issue.

Sometimes the columnist suggests they seek counseling to discuss issues in an unbiased manner. The fact is people are looking for guidance on how to deal with issues in their lives. There is guidance available from a great source. It just takes discipline to use it, because it is our tendency to try to solve our own problems. The source is a several inch-thick collection of books written thousands of years ago, but appropriate today.

The Bible provides passages to deal with specific problems in life, and most come with a reference guide showing appropriate passages based on keywords. My Bible has a Concordance that tells where to find passages addressing the keywords of any dilemma. You can find all kinds of inexpensive paperback topical reference guides that point you to specific scripture verses. You can also type into your browser, "Scripture verses about ____," and you can find God's Word and even sermons about any topic or question. The information is right at your fingertips.

Friends are also where you can go to in times of trouble. Friends love you and want what is best for you. They understand the context and personalities of what you are dealing with. Keep in mind, however, that their guidance may be more what they think you want to hear. If you have read many Dear Amy columns you probably realize that sometimes the person writing to Amy is the one who has the unrealistic expectations. If that person's confidant merely tells them what they want to hear, the advice won't be the right answer. Value friends immensely, but value God's perfect guidance more. God's advice is what is right for all time, not just what will make you feel good today.

A key element to dealing with issues is prayer. Make this a time when you stop talking and listen for God's answer. This is when God shows His understanding of the context of your situation as He plants in your mind what He wants you to do. For people who like to be in control of everything, that kind of prayer is difficult. But if you want to know God's solution, you must listen.

Make God's Word your starting place:

When in sorrow, read *John 14*
When other people fail you, read *Psalm 27*
When you have sinned, read *Psalm 51*
When you worry, read, *Matthew 6:19-34*
When God seems far away, read *Psalm 139*
When your faith needs stirring, read *Hebrews 11*
When you are lonely and fearful, read *Psalm 23*
When you grow bitter and critical, read *1 Corinthians 13*
When you feel down and out, read *Romans 8:31*
When you want courage for a task, read *Joshua 1*
When you are depressed, read *Psalm 27*
When you are afraid of stepping out of your comfort zone, read *Philippians 4:13*.
When you are losing confidence in people, read *1 Corinthians 13*
When you are discouraged about your work, read *Psalm 126*

Make it a three-step approach: After reading the passage, go to the Lord in prayer and listen for his voice helping you with your specific situation. Then talk with your friends for their support of God's direction for your life. Their desire to do what is best for you will now be guided by God's plan for you. As a result, you have God's direction and a local support base.

My prayer for you is that you will be surrounded by loving family and friends but you will anchor your life decisions with God's word.

Question:	In what ways can you focus on understanding God's direction for the issues we face? How can you engage trusted friends to support God's plan.

Prayer:	Lord, You are our anchor in good times and bad. We pray we will focus our attention on Your guidance for our lives. Amen.

Topic: Easter

The Fulfillment of History at Easter – Some Aha Moments

I am sure you have played hide and seek, either inside or outside the house. After looking high and low you finally discover the hidden person, and say, "Aha. There you are." The study of Holy Week events provide us with newly found "aha moments," adding a deeper meaning to the Passion of the Christ.

We often take for granted the events of Easter week. We live in a modern culture while the events of Easter week happened two thousand years ago. We need to better understand the culture of its time.

It is easy to hear the accounts of Holy Week and not fully realize the significance and God's precision timing of the events. Sometimes the meaning of what happened is hidden from us. Then it hits us. "Aha."

"Aha moments" are supposed to give us the feeling – oh, wow – so that is what it is all about. I never thought of things that way. A deeper understanding will help us focus on what they mean in our lives.

Aha Moment #1: When Jesus entered Jerusalem on the final week he did it to coincide with the Jewish tradition of his time. The day we call Palm Sunday was "Lamb Selection Day" in the Jewish tradition of its time. Families selected a perfect lamb to be sacrificed at the celebration of Passover, which would occur five days later. **God timed Jesus' entry into Jerusalem, just before Passover, as His way of saying, "Here is my perfect lamb for the sacrifice."**

Aha Moment #2: It was the custom in the Jewish faith that at 3 PM on the first day of Passover, a horn would sound and a lamb would be sacrificed. On the first day of Passover, Jesus was nailed to the cross. At 3 PM on Good Friday, Jesus lifted up his head, said "It is finished," and died. The exact timing of his death matched the tradition of the time when lambs were sacrificed. **God saw to it that his son, the Lamb of God, was sacrificed at the exact time of the Passover tradition.**

Aha Moment #3: What was happening at the time when Jesus entered the city on Palm Sunday? Large crowds had gathered in Jerusalem for the Passover. Passover is a historical celebration of the story of Exodus, when the Israelites were freed from slavery in Egypt. The entire Jewish population made a pilgrimage to Jerusalem each year for the Passover festival. At the time of Jesus entry into Jerusalem there was no cause to celebrate. The people were no longer free, but instead were under oppressive Roman rule. Previous year's riots put the Roman soldiers on high alert during the Passover celebration. When we wave palm branches in our modern church on Palm Sunday we think of it as a celebration. But actuality, the waving of Palm branches was a political statement, like waving your country's flag in the face of unfriendly rulers. The chanting of "Hosanna" was a thorn in the side of the Roman rulers. We think of it as a joyful chant in modern times, but at the time it meant "deliver me," or free me. **The lamb who preached peace and love was in the middle of an event with the very opposite purpose.** The people wanted Jesus to overthrow the Romans. That is certainly not why he came. Jesus wanted us to overthrow Satan in our lives.

Aha Moment #4: Fast forward now to Thursday evening, which we call Maundy Thursday. In Jewish law festivals begin at sundown the night before. Thursday evening was the night before Passover. After dining with his disciples in The Upper Room Jesus poured out a cup of wine and said the familiar words we hear at communion in our own modern churches. The disciples had heard these words before, but in a totally different context. In Jesus' time, when a young man wanted to ask for a women's hand in marriage, the tradition was for the young man's father to pour out a cup of wine, and hand it to his son. The son would then offer it to the young woman saying, "This cup is a new covenant in my blood, which I offer to you." If the young woman accepted, she would take the cup and drink from it. In other words, the man was saying, **"I love you and I'll give you my life.** Will you marry me?" And, by taking the cup, the young woman's action said, "I accept your offer, and I give you my life in response. At the Last Supper, Jesus made a covenant proposal to his disciples. In effect, He said, "I love you, and I offer my life, for you." Jesus makes this proposal to you and me, also. We have the option of whether or not to accept, take the cup, and give our life to Christ, in response to his love.

Aha Moment #5: And, on resurrection day, the Bible tells us Jesus exited the tomb before the stone was rolled away. Moving the stone allowed man to enter the tomb and see that Jesus was no longer there; He had risen. The resurrection fulfilled the promise Jesus would rise in three days. **The resurrection provided living proof of God's commitment to raise believers from the dead – all who believe in Him (Romans 10:9).**

And, we can remember his proposal to us at the communion rail. "This cup is a new covenant in my blood." Jesus did this because of his love for us. Do you accept Jesus' offer?

Question:	Jesus is offering you the cup of redemption. Do you accept His offer?
Scripture:	*In Christ we are set free by the blood of his death, and so we have forgiveness of sins (Ephesians 1:7).*
Prayer:	We thank you, Lord, for the sacrifice of your son, Jesus Christ, so we may be forgiven of our sins. Amen.

The aha moments of this summary are based on a Ray Vander Laan video titled The True Easter Story.

Topic: Helping One
Another

Surrounded by Wisdom

 **Who is your favorite Biblical character?** What person in the Bible inspired you the most, perhaps by stepping out in faith to do something great? What would you ask that person if you were to meet face-to-face? Since that meeting won't occur until the next life, look for Biblical passages to see how they were able to accomplish what they did. Chances are they relied on the strength of God working through them. *I can do all this through him who gives me strength (Philippians 4:13).*

Want to learn how to play outstanding basketball? Spend some time with a person who exhibits the skills you want to develop. Learn from being around them.

What person in the community would you most like to talk with about what made them successful? Ask to mentor with them for a few days so you can learn from the best. *Walk with the wise and become wise, for a companion of fools suffers harm (Proverbs 13:20).*

What family member inspires you to accomplish more than

you thought possible? They know you the best this side of Heaven. Listen to their wisdom and step out of your comfort zone and give it a try. *Listen, my son, to your father's instruction and do not forsake your mother's teaching (Proverbs 1:8).*

Do you admire someone's spirituality in the midst of chaos? Ask them how they feel the peace and presence of God in spite of living in this challenging world. *And the peace of God, which transcends all understanding, will guard your hearts and your minds in Christ Jesus (Philippians 4:7).*

We are all influenced by other people, positively or negatively. What wisdom could they impart on us? Be open to exploring in order to become the person you really want to be. Take advantage of the wisdom and positive influences all around you.

It is all about the company we keep. Family members give a reason for living and they influence the choices we make. People – family and community – have a great impact on the language we use, our outlook on life, and our willingness to help others. If your friends make poor choices, you may also. *Do not be misled: Bad company corrupts good character (1 Corinthians 15:33).* However, if the people around you "walk the talk" of their faith, you will too. The choice is yours.

You can help in your circle of family and friends. A healthy relationship goes both ways. When someone else is feeling down you can lift them up, and they will do the same for you when you need encouragement. *If either of them falls down, one can help the other up. But pity anyone who falls and has no one to help them up (Ecclesiastes 4:10).* Without a supportive environment there would be no one to encourage you.

Being in the presence of people of faith will create all the difference in the world in the kind of person you are. You won't have the exact same spiritual gifts as someone else, but you can be inspired by their spirit for the Lord. Surround yourself with the spiritually wise, and you can accomplish great things in His name.

Prayer: We thank You, Lord, for placing people in our lives that can be a great influence on us. Open our hearts and minds to the right influences so we can be all You made us to be. Amen.

The following two pages give additional scriptural eamples of Biblical mentors.

Bruce Boyer

Biblical Examples of Mentors

Jethro mentoring Moses *Exodus 18:1, 6-27*

Moses mentoring Joshua *Exodus 17:9*

Jesus mentoring his disciples throughout the New Testament

Barnabas mentoring Paul *Acts 9:26-30, Acts 4:36, Acts 11, 13*

Paul mentoring Timothy, Silvanus & Titus *Corinthians 1:1, 1 Thessalonians 1:1 Galatians 3:1*

Elizabeth mentoring Mary (the mother of Jesus *Luke 1:26-46*

Naomi mentoring Ruth *Ruth 1:16-17*

Note: The Bible does not use the term mentor, but there are clearly mentoring in these biblical relationships.

Additional Scripture Passages

Mentoring Friends:

Do you not know that your bodies are temples of the Holy Spirit, who is in you, whom you have received from God? You are not your own; you were bought at a price. Therefore honor God with your bodies (1 Corinthians 6:19-20).

As iron sharpens iron, so one person sharpens another (Proverbs 27:17).

One generation commends your works to another; they tell of your mighty acts (Psalms 145:4).

Mentoring Within the Family:

Start children off on the way they should go, and even when they are old they will not turn from it (Proverbs 22:6).

Bruce Boyer

The Gift of Health

Imagine this scenario. Two neighbors both receive an anonymous gift of a luxury car. The new cars are identical with all of the bells and whistles, a high performance engine, a sleek and attractive design. What a wonderful, free gift.

One of the neighbors takes prudent care of his car, washing it frequently, changing the oil on schedule, and faithfully complying with all of the service plan recommendations. The other, however, drives the car frequently but does nothing to maintain it. Too busy doing other things. The once beautiful car quickly declines in its value.

Fast forward a few years and compare the condition of each car. The well-maintained car looks and sounds great. It performs well on the road and still turns heads in the neighborhood. The neglected car is a different story. You can actually hear it coming down the street, the motor laboring, and the valves clicking, a dead giveaway of its poor maintenance. Luckily, this car is parked in the

259

garage because it looks unsightly, needing both a wash and wax job to try to restore its former luster. It is too late to restore it mechanically even if you replace the engine and most of its components. The lifespan and usefulness of each car differs significantly.

At birth God gave you a perfect luxury body, with all the possible features you could ever want. Your birth was a one-time gift with a warranty only valid if you followed the service plan. Did you park it on the sofa? Did you follow the well-documented service plan of regular exercise and healthy living, or did you feed it with junk food? Were you too busy to maintain your body?

Research over the years has clearly given us an owner's manual for our body, recommending the fuel and exercise plan that keeps us as healthy as possible. Don't let the busyness of life rob you of the opportunity to be a well-balanced, healthy person.

Be thankful for the gift of health, as it is a gift from God. God gave you this gift for a reason. A well-tuned body gives you maximum opportunity to serve Him – in your families, in the workplace, and in the community. Take care of your body by choosing a healthy lifestyle. After all, God lives within you, hoping you use it to further His Kingdom. *So whether you eat or drink or whatever you do, do it all for the glory of God (1 Corinthians 10:31).*

If you treat your body with respect and honor, God will more likely reward you with good health and healing. *Nevertheless, I will bring health and healing to it; I will heal my people and will let them enjoy abundant peace and security (Jeremiah 33:6).*

So, how do we do this when there is so much pressure to produce at work and maintain the fast pace of life our world seems to require? Consider these thoughts:

What are the priorities God wants for your life? God doesn't want the frantic pace of life that threatens your health and keeps you from serving Him. Seek better balance in your life.

Know that if you are healthy your production at work will improve. Your capacity will increase so you can do more with less time. You'll be a better employee.

Develop an exercise plan and stick with it. There will be days when excuses take you out of your routine. Once you give in to an excuse, another will soon come up. Before you know it you are back to your old, unhealthy habits of neglect. If you are too busy to exercise, you desperately need it more than anyone because your stress level is probably through the roof.

Find someone else who can hold you accountable to your promise to make an effort to improve your health habits. You can mutually be an encourager with others. *Therefore encourage one another and build each other up, just as in fact you are doing (1 Thessalonians 5:11).*

Keep worship in your schedule. You have much to be thankful for, and that thanks goes to God. He may hear your prayers from the couch but he will respect the sincerity of your prayers from His house of worship. Ask God to keep you strong in your commitment to health. You need His help to change old habits.

Rest on the Sabbath. *Remember the Sabbath day by keeping it holy. Six days you shall labor and do all your work, but the seventh day is a Sabbath to the LORD your God. On it you shall not do any work (Exodus 20:8).*

Eat, drink and do things in **moderation** so that you enjoy life, but will enjoy it longer. *But the fruit of the Spirit is love, joy, peace, forbearance, kindness, goodness, faithfulness, gentleness and self-control. Against such things there is no law (Galatians 5:22-23).*

Worried about your ability to support your family, causing you to put pressure on yourself at work? God promises abundance, but to those who show an effort to be **good stewards** of this gift. *Moreover, when God gives someone wealth and possessions, and the ability to enjoy them, to accept their lot and be happy in their toil—this is a gift of God (Ecclesiastes 5:19).*

You have much to live for, especially your family who loves you and counts on you to be there for them. Your family is also a gift from God, deserving of your best. *Every good and perfect gift is from above, coming down from the Father of the heavenly lights, who does not change like shifting shadows (James 1:17).*

So, which car do you want: the neglected car on the fast track to the junkyard or the well-kept car that will perform well for many years to come? It is up to you, at least until that decision is taken away from you by your body, revolting from the abuse of poor choices.

Question: What can you do to take care of your body so that you will be able to fully serve Him?

Prayer: Dear Lord, it is easy to get swept up in the pace of life, the desire to succeed, and the excuses we make to not fully take care of ourselves. We pray we will honor the gift of health You gave us at birth. Amen.

Bruce Boyer

Topic: Mentoring

Everyone Is in Need
of a Mentor

Every day we hear stories about athletes, actors, and other public figures that have made bad decisions. Being athletically gifted, talented at acting, or financially well off doesn't mean a person has it together when it comes to life choices. Being rich or famous makes you rich or famous, but has no correlation with having a rich spiritual life.

Just think how much better off the rich and famous would be if they had a personal advisor who was more concerned with the Bible instead of the balance sheet. Instead of telling someone what they want to hear, a spiritual mentor would tell them what they need to hear.

Few of us can be categorized as rich and famous, but we all face issues: ethical decisions, relationship issues, or other personal issues. We may also question our self-esteem. That certainly is the case with young people trying to establish their own identities. The quest for self-esteem based on the world often drives our life decisions.

Compared to the models and actors featured in advertisements, we don't all have slim bodies and full heads of hair. We may wish we looked like someone else and go to extreme measures seeking to be what we aren't. We don't realize it is OK to be the person God made us to be. Scripture tells us we are wonderfully made *(Psalm 139:14)*.

People need a mentor, especially with the pressures of today's world. A mentor helps you:

• Seek examples of others living by Godly principles -- people who can best lead by example if they are living by Christ's example *(Titus 2:6)*.

• Hear the right answers to your issues, not just what others think you want to hear *(Proverbs 27:17)*.

• Talk with others who have experienced pain and overcome the issues of life *(Psalm 145:4)*.

• Know, in spite of your own shortcomings, that others believe in you *(2 Thessalonians 5:11)*.

• Have confidence to go on in life and not give in to easy solutions that actually bring more pain *(Philippians 4:13)*.

• Be an example for others to follow once you have risen above your issues *(1 Peter 5:2-3)*. With Godly wisdom, you can be a mentor for others.

Seek the friendship of someone you admire that exhibits faith in their daily life, and let them be a light to guide you. Keep in mind human mentors are just that – human. Understand their answers are not perfect, but if they are based on the Bible, Godly advice is perfect. The apostle Paul said, *Follow my example, as I follow the example of Christ (1 Corinthians 11:1)*.

As you grow, seek opportunities to share your spiritual growth with others. When you do, be a good example yourself: *In everything set them an example by doing what is good. In your teaching show integrity, seriousness and soundness of speech that cannot be condemned, so that those who oppose you may be ashamed because they have nothing bad to say about us (Titus 2:7-8).*

The voice of our earthly culture is not biblical. Instead, choose the voice of a Christian mentor. They share God's answer to the issues of your life. Mentors help people reach the potential God had intended for them.

Question: How can you be a mentor to someone else?

Prayer: Lord, you gave us the answers in the Bible and the life of Jesus. Let us follow Jesus as we help others to find their way. Amen.

Mentoring Scripture References from the Story:

• *I praise you because I am fearfully and wonderfully made; your works are wonderful, I know that full well (Psalm 139:14).*

• *Similarly, encourage the young men to be self-controlled (Titus 2:6).*

• *But the fruit of the Spirit is love, joy, peace, forbearance, kindness, goodness, faithfulness, gentleness and self-control. Against such things there is no law. Those who belong to Christ Jesus have crucified the flesh with its passions and desires (Galatians 5:22-24).*

• *As iron sharpens iron, so one person sharpens another (Proverbs 27:17).*

• *One generation commends your works to another; they tell of your mighty acts (Proverbs 145:4).*

• *Therefore encourage one another and build each other up, just as in fact you are doing (2 Thessalonians 5:11).*

• *I can do all this through him who gives me strength (Philippians 4:13).*

• *Be shepherds of God's flock that is under your care, watching over them— not because you must, but because you are willing, as God wants you to be; not pursuing dishonest gain, but eager to serve; not lording it over those entrusted to you, but being examples to the flock (1 Peter 5:2-3).*

Topic: Tools to Help
Solve Problems

Tools of Faith

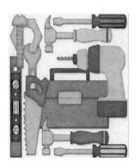

We recently cleaned out the garage, literally going through everything, including the contents of our portable tool box. We mounted as many tools as possible on the pegboard above the workbench, making them easier to find. Without the right tools it is a struggle to get a project done. I can't tell you how many times I have gone to the garage seeking the right tool, and leaving in frustration because it wasn't where I could find it. But now, the garage is organized so that I can find what I need.

My daughter teaches voice lessons in New York City. Because Kara is a good listener and grounded in her faith, many of her students share their personal problems with her. Kara remarked to me recently many people lack the tools to deal with issues they are facing. Often they are focused on getting their way or "getting even" with someone. In these cases, their focus is only on themselves, not on resolving the problem. In effect, selfish actions will only make the problem worse. People of faith have many more tools available to reach a mutual agreement because they seek a solution pleasing to the Heavenly Father, seeking God's answers.

Here are some key tools provided by a faith in God that seeks solutions pleasing to God:

1. **Prayer:** Ask God to be the center of your life; ask God for answers to issues you face.

2. **Christian friends:** Christian friends can give Godly advice. Non-Christians are more likely to tell you what they think you want to hear. Christian advice is what God knows you need to hear.

3. **Pastoral and/or Christian counseling:** When resolution of issues is particularly difficult, Christian counseling can help you sort through issues and give a clear direction and a plan to deal with problems.

4. **The Word of God, the Bible**, gives clear direction and answers not only on what is the right thing to do, but how to work through relationship issues with others.

> a. The 10 Commandments clearly outline
> > (1) our relationship with God and
>
> > (2) our relationship with each other.
>
> b. Scripture verses relate to specific issues you may be facing or relationship issues with others.
>
> c. Internet resources:

Just Google your question, "What does God say about _____," will give you the rationale behind God's Word. Or Google "scripture verses about _____" to find actual biblical references for the topic of your query. You don't need to be a Bible scholar to find the answers.

5. **Love:** God loves us. Everything, especially relationships, is based on His love for us. If we work through issues showing God's love, our solutions to life issues will be much different. And

so will the results.

Understand that God thinks differently than we do. Often His answers are directly in contrast to what our world tells us to do. We live in a sinful world, whose motives are different than God's motives. We can trust God for the right answers. God provides us with the tools to live in loving relationships with each other. Following His guidelines will reduce stress and steer us away from negative ways to handle situations.

When searching for tools to deal with relationship issues, focus on these areas: Love, Forgiveness, and Strength. Below are a few key references for each.

Love: The greatest commandment is to love thy neighbor as yourself.

- *Do to others as you would have them do to you (Luke 6:31).*

- *But love your enemies, do good to them, and lend to them without expecting to get anything back. Then your reward will be great, and you will be children of the Most High, because he is kind to the ungrateful and wicked (Luke 6:35).*

- *Love must be sincere. Hate what is evil; cling to what is good (Romans 12:9).*

- *The second is this: 'Love your neighbor as yourself.' There is no commandment greater than these (Mark 12:31).*

- *This is how we know what love is: Jesus Christ laid down his life for us. And we ought to lay down our lives for our brothers and sisters. If anyone has material possessions and sees a brother or sister in need but has no pity on them, how can the love of God be in that person? Dear children, let us not love with words or speech but with actions and in truth (1 John 3:16-18).*

- *Whoever does not love does not know God, because God is love (1 John 4:8).*

- *For God so loved the world that he gave his one and only Son, that whoever believes in him shall not perish but have eternal life (John 3:16).*

• *Love is patient, love is kind. It does not envy, it does not boast, it is not proud. It does not dishonor others, it is not self-seeking, it is not easily angered, it keeps no record of wrongs. Love does not delight in evil but rejoices with the truth. It always protects, always trusts, always hopes, always perseveres (1 Corinthians 13:4-7).*

• *And now these three remain: faith, hope and love. But the greatest of these is love (1 Corinthians 13:13).*

• *Be completely humble and gentle; be patient, bearing with one another in love (Ephesians 4:2).*

• *Above all, love each other deeply, because love covers over a multitude of sins (1 Peter 4:8).*

• *Dear friends, let us love one another, for love comes from God. Everyone who loves has been born of God and knows God (1 John 4:7).*

• *There is no fear in love. But perfect love drives out fear, because fear has to do with punishment. The one who fears is not made perfect in love. We love because he first loved us (1 John 4:18-19).*

• *Greater love has no one than this: to lay down one's life for one's friends (John 15:13).*

• *Husbands, love your wives, just as Christ loved the church and gave himself up for her (Ephesians 5:25).*

• *However, each one of you also must love his wife as he loves himself, and the wife must respect her husband (Ephesians 5:33).*

• *Hatred stirs up conflict, but love covers over all wrongs (Proverbs 10:12).*

Forgiveness: A key tool to be able to forgive others and to forgive yourself.

• *For if you forgive other people when they sin against you, your heavenly Father will also forgive you. But if you do not forgive others their sins, your Father will not forgive your sins (Matthew 6:14-15).*

• *If we confess our sins, he is faithful and just and will forgive us our sins and purify us from all unrighteousness (1 John 1:9).*

• *Repent, then, and turn to God, so that your sins may be wiped out, that times of refreshing may come from the Lord (Acts 3:19).*

• *In him we have redemption through his blood, the forgiveness of sins, in accordance with the riches of God's grace (Ephesians 1:7).*

•*As a father has compassion on his children, so the LORD has compassion on those who fear him (Psalms 103:13).*

•*For if you forgive other people when they sin against you, your heavenly Father will also forgive you. But if you do not forgive others their sins, your Father will not forgive your sins (Matthew 6:14-15).*

•*And when you stand praying, if you hold anything against anyone, forgive them, so that your Father in heaven may forgive you your sins (Mark 11:25).*

Strength: We need the strength to withstand temptations and to utilize God's power to help us overcome situations.

• *He gives strength to the weary and increases the power of the weak (Isaiah 40:29).*

• *I can do all this through him who gives me strength (Philippians 4:13).*

• *Finally, be strong in the Lord and in his mighty power (Ephesians 6:10).*

• *But who hope in the LORD will renew their strength; they will soar on wings like eagles; they will run and not grow weary, they will walk and not be faint (Isaiah 40:31).*

• *But he said to me, "My grace is sufficient for you, for my power is made perfect in weakness." Therefore I will boast all the more gladly about my weaknesses, so that Christ's power may rest on me (2 Corinthians 12:9).*

• *God is our refuge and strength, an ever-present help in trouble (Psalms 46:1).*

• *The LORD is my strength and my shield; my heart trusts in him, and he helps me. My heart leaps for joy, and with my song I praise him. The LORD is the strength of his people, a fortress of salvation for his anointed one (Psalm 28:7-8).*

• *The LORD is my strength and my defense; he has become my salvation (Psalm 118:14).*

• *Surely God is my salvation; I will trust and not be afraid. The LORD, the LORD himself, is my strength and my defense; he has become my salvation (Isaiah 12:2).*

• *LORD, be gracious to us; we long for you. Be our strength every morning, our salvation in time of distress (Isaiah 33:2).*

• *I pray that out of his glorious riches he may strengthen you with power through his Spirit in your inner being (Ephesians 3:16).*

Be guided by scripture. Go to the Lord in prayer, ask him to give you the strength to forgive and treat others in love. Those are tools of faith that will help you deal with relationships and move forward in the path God will lay out for you.

Question: What tools do you use to discern God's answers to the issues you face?

Prayer: Heavenly Father, life throws all kinds of challenges at us. When we have disagreements, we pray we will seek Your guidance and treat others with love and respect. Amen.

Topical Scripture References

This is a quick reference guide of scripture verses relating to God's blessings, promises to us and the issues we may face in our life. This is not an exhaustive list, but an excellent starting point. For more Biblical references about a specific topic, just type into your browser, "what does scripture say about _____" and a wealth of appropriate verses will be immediately available to you. We don't have to face life alone. God has answers to all our concerns. All verses are from the NIV Bible.

Anger

• *In your anger do not sin: Do not let the sun go down while you are still angry, and do not give the devil a foothold (Ephesians 4:26-27).*

Belief

• *For God so loved the world that he gave his one and only Son, that whoever believes in him shall not perish but have eternal life (John 3:16).*

• *I have come into the world as a light, so that no one who believes in me should stay in darkness (John 12:46).*

• *Then Jesus declared, "I am the bread of life. Whoever comes to me will never go hungry, and whoever believes in me will never be thirsty (John 6:35).*

• *They replied, "Believe in the Lord Jesus, and you will be saved—you and your household" (Acts 16:31).*

Blessings

• *Every good and perfect gift is from above, coming down from the Father of the heavenly lights, who does not change like shifting shadows (James 1:17).*

• *For there is no difference between Jew and Gentile—the same Lord is Lord of all and richly blesses all who call on him for, "Everyone who calls on the name of the Lord will be saved" (Romans 10:12-13).*

Charity

• *The generous will themselves be blessed, for they share their food with the poor (Proverbs 22:9).*

• *Jesus looked at him and loved him. "One thing you lack," he said. "Go, sell everything you have and give to the poor, and you will have treasure in heaven. Then come, follow me" (Mark 10:21).*

Children

• *When Jesus saw this, he was indignant. He said to them, "Let the little children come to me, and do not hinder them, for the kingdom of God belongs to such as these. Truly I tell you, anyone who will not receive the kingdom of God like a little child will never enter it." And he took the children in his arms, placed his hands on them and blessed them (Mark 10:14-16).*

• *Children, obey your parents in everything, for this pleases the Lord (Colossians 3:20).*

• *You know the commandments: 'You shall not commit adultery, you shall not murder, you shall not steal, you shall not give false testimony, honor your father and mother' (Luke 18:20).*

Comfort

• *God is our refuge and strength, an ever-present help in trouble (Psalm 46:1).*

• *Come to me, all you who are weary and burdened, and I will give you rest" (Matthew 11:28).*

• *Even though I walk through the darkest valley I will fear no evil, for you are with me; your rod and your staff, they comfort me (Psalm 23:4).*

Conflict

• *Do not repay anyone evil for evil. Be careful to do what is right in the eyes of everyone. If it is possible, as far as it depends on you, live at peace with everyone (Romans 12:17-18).*

• *Blessed are the peacemakers, for they will be called children of God (Matthew 5:9).*

Contentment

• *Let us not become conceited, provoking and envying each other (Galatians 5:26).*

• *Peace I leave with you; my peace I give you. I do not give to you as the world gives. Do not let your hearts be troubled and do not be afraid (John 14:27).*

Courage

• *I know what it is to be in need, and I know what it is to have plenty. I have learned the secret of being content in any and every situation, whether well fed or hungry, whether living in plenty or in want. I can do all this through him who gives me strength (Philippians 4:12-13).*

• *For the Spirit God gave us does not make us timid, but gives us power, love and self-discipline (2 Timothy 1:7).*

Discouragement

• *Let us not become weary in doing good, for at the proper time we will reap a harvest if we do not give up (Galatians 6:9).*

Eternal Life

- *Very truly I tell you, the one who believes has eternal life (John 6:47).*

- *My sheep listen to my voice; I know them, and they follow me. I give them eternal life, and they shall never perish; no one will snatch them out of my hand (John 10:27-28).*

- *Jesus said to her, "I am the resurrection and the life. The one who believes in me will live, even though they die; and whoever lives by believing in me will never die. Do you believe this?"*

Faith

- *Now faith is confidence in what we hope for and assurance about what we do not see (Hebrews 11:1).*

- *I have fought the good fight, I have finished the race, I have kept the faith (2 Timothy 4:7).*

Fear

- *"Do not be afraid, little flock, for your Father has been pleased to give you the kingdom" (Luke 12:32).*

- *The LORD is my light and my salvation, whom shall I fear? The LORD is the stronghold of my life, of whom shall I be afraid? (Psalm 27:1).*

Forgiveness

- *But I tell you, love your enemies and pray for those who persecute you ... (Matthew 5:44).*

- *"Do not judge, and you will not be judged. Do not condemn, and you will not be condemned. Forgive, and you will be forgiven" (Luke 6:37).*

- *If we confess our sins, he is faithful and just and will forgive us our sins and purify us from all unrighteousness (1 John 1:9).*

Fruitfulness

- *But the fruit of the Spirit is love, joy, peace, forbearance, kindness, good-*

ness, faithfulness, gentleness and self-control. Against such things there is no law (Galatians 5:22-23).

Grace

• *For it is by grace you have been saved, through faith—and this is not from yourselves, it is the gift of God— not by works, so that no one can boast (Ephesians 2:8-9).*

Gossip

• *May these words of my mouth and this meditation of my heart be pleasing in your sight, LORD, my Rock and my Redeemer (Psalm 19:14).*

• *Keep your tongue from evil and your lips from telling lies (Psalm 34:13).*

Guidance

• *I will instruct you and teach you in the way you should go; I will counsel you with my loving eye on you (Psalm 32:8).*

• *For this God is our God for ever and ever; he will be our guide even to the end (Psalm 48:14).*

• *Trust in the LORD with all your heart and lean not on your own understanding; in all your ways submit to him, and he will make your paths straight (Proverbs 3:5-6).*

Help

• *Though he may stumble, he will not fall, for the LORD upholds him with his hand (Psalm 37:24).*

Hope

• *For you have been my hope, Sovereign LORD, my confidence since my youth (Psalm 71:5).*

• *Be strong and take heart, all you who hope in the LORD (Psalm 31:24).*

Humility

• *Let someone else praise you, and not your own mouth; an outsider, and not your own lips (Proverbs 27:2).*

• *Therefore, whoever takes the lowly position of this child is the greatest in the kingdom of heaven (Matthew 18:4).*

• *For those who exalt themselves will be humbled, and those who humble themselves will be exalted (Matthew 23:12).*

Joy

• *I have told you this so that my joy may be in you and that your joy may be complete (John 15:11).*

• *In him our hearts rejoice, for we trust in his holy name (Psalm 33:21).*

Love

• *No, the Father himself loves you because you have loved me and have believed that I came from God (John 16:27).*

• *We love because he first loved us (1 John 4:19).*

• *A new command I give you: Love one another. As I have loved you, so you must love one another. By this everyone will know that you are my disciples, if you love one another" (John 13:34-35).*

Mercy

• *The LORD is gracious and compassionate; slow to anger and rich in love. The LORD is good to all; he has compassion on all he has made (Psalm 145:8-9).*

• *As a father has compassion on his children, so the LORD has compassion on those who fear him (Psalm 103:13).*

• *His mercy extends to those who fear him, from generation to generation (Luke 1:50).*

Mistakes

• *Whoever conceals their sins does not prosper, but the one who confesses and renounces them finds mercy (Proverbs 28:13).*

Obedience

• *And we know that in all things God works for the good of those who love him, who have been called according to his purpose. (Romans 8:28).*

• *If you keep my commands, you will remain in my love, just as I have kept my Father's commands and remain in his love (John 15:10).*

Past, The

• *Brothers and sisters, I do not consider myself yet to have taken hold of it. But one thing I do: Forgetting what is behind and straining toward what is ahead, 14 I press on toward the goal to win the prize for which God has called me heavenward in Christ Jesus (Philippians 3:13-14).*

• *And we know that in all things God works for the good of those who love him, who have been called according to his purpose (Romans 8:28).*

Patience

• *Not only so, but we also glory in our sufferings, because we know that suffering produces perseverance; perseverance, character; and character, hope (Romans 5:3-4).*

• *You need to persevere so that when you have done the will of God, you will receive what he has promised (Hebrews 10:36).*

Peace

• *And the peace of God, which transcends all understanding, will guard yourhearts and our minds in Christ Jesus (Philippians 4:7).*

• *You will keep in perfect peace those whose minds are steadfast, because they trust in you (Isaiah 26:3).*

Prayer

• *Ask and it will be given to you; seek and you will find; knock and the door will be opened to you. For everyone who asks receives; the one who seeks finds; and to the one who knocks, the door will be opened (Matthew 7:7-8).*

- *If you believe, you will receive whatever you ask for in prayer (Matthew 21:22).*

- *Rejoice always, pray continually, give thanks in all circumstances; for this is God's will for you in Christ Jesus (1 Thessalonians 5:16-18).*

Rest

- *Remember the Sabbath day by keeping it holy. Six days you shall labor and do all your work, but the seventh day is a Sabbath to the LORD your God. On it you shall not do any work, neither you, nor your son or daughter, nor your male or female servant, nor your animals, nor any foreigner residing in your towns. For in six days the LORD made the heavens and the earth, the sea, and all that is in them, but he rested on the seventh day. Therefore the LORD blessed the Sabbath day and made it holy.*

Righteousness

- *But seek first his kingdom and his righteousness, and all these things will be given to you as well (Matthew 6:33).*

- *Surely your goodness and love will follow me all the days of my life, and I will dwell in the house of the LORD forever (Psalm 23:6).*

Strength

- *God is our protection and our strength. He always helps in times of trouble …The Lord All-Powerful is with us; the God of Jacob is our defender (Psalm 46:1, 11).*

- *He gives strength to those who are tired and more power to those who are weak … But the people who trust the Lord will become strong again. They will rise up as an eagle in the sky; they will run and not need rest; they will walk and not become tired (Isaiah 40: 29, 31).*

Success

- *That each of them may eat and drink, and find satisfaction in all their toil—this is the gift of God (Ecclesiastes 3:13).*

Trust

• *Trust in the LORD with all your heart and lean not on your own understanding; in all your ways submit to him, and he will make your paths straight (Proverbs 3:5-6).*

Wisdom

• *If any of you lacks wisdom, you should ask God, who gives generously to all without finding fault, and it will be given to you (James 1:5).*

• *Many peoples will come and say, come, let us go up to the mountain of the LORD, to the temple of the God of Jacob. He will teach us his ways, so that we may walk in his paths." The law will go out from Zion, the word of the LORD from Jerusalem (Isaiah 2:3).*

Worry

• *Do not be anxious about anything, but in every situation, by prayer and petition, with thanksgiving, present your requests to God. 7 And the peace of God, which transcends all understanding, will guard your hearts and your minds in Christ Jesus (Philippians 4:6-7).*

• *God is our refuge and strength, an ever-present help in trouble. Therefore we will not fear, though the earth give way and the mountains fall into the heart of the sea, though its waters roar and foam and the mountains quake with their surging (Psalms 46:1-3).*

• *Cast all your anxiety on him because he cares for you (1 Peter 5:7).*

• *Do not let your hearts be troubled. You believe in God; believe also in me (John 14:1).*

Bruce Boyer

About the Author

Bruce Boyer is an author of Christian short stories, having previously published <u>24/7 – Stories of Faith from Everyday Life</u> in 2015. His own personal ministry involves publishing devotional stories each week on his devotional website, www.ChristianFaith-Stories.com. Devotional story lines draw upon his 34 years of professional YMCA experience and observations from everyday life. For the past 30 years Bruce has worked nationally as a representative for the Walker Foundation at Christian Leadership conferences. In addition, he has started and directed CLC's at 3 different YMCA's around the country. His passion for the YMCA's Christian mission dramatically increased after his son was miraculously rescued from being lost six days in the Amazon rainforest of Brazil. Only God could have orchestrated that dramatic rescue. The devotional books Bruce has written are his response to God's grace in saving his son.

I will give thanks to you, LORD, with all my heart; I will tell of all your wonderful deeds (Psalm 9:1).

For More Stories of Faith by Bruce Boyer

Visit www.ChristianFaithStories.com

CPSIA information can be obtained
at www.ICGtesting.com
Printed in the USA
FFOW02n0035151216
30172FF